Spending
Smarter

UNIVERSITY OF WINNIPEG

JAN 27 REC'D

DEAN OF ARTS & SCIENCE

Spending Smarter

Corporate-University Cooperation in Research and Development

J.V. RAYMOND CYR
Chairman
Forum Task Force

CORPORATE-HIGHER EDUCATION FORUM

©Corporate-Higher Education Forum 1985
All rights reserved.

Extracts of up to 200 words may be reproduced without permission. Acknowledgement of source is requested and should read: "Reprinted by permission of the Corporate-Higher Education Forum". Permission to reproduce extracts longer than 200 words should be referred to:

Corporate-Higher Education Forum
1155 Dorchester Blvd. West, Suite 2501
Montreal, Quebec H3B 2K4

ISBN 0-920429-04-1

Canadian cataloguing in publication data

Cyr, J.V. Raymond (Joseph Victor Raymond) 1934
Spending smarter: corporate-university co-operation in r & d

Published also in French under title: Investir plus sagement
Bibliography: p.
ISBN 0-920429-04-1

1. Science and industry—Canada   2. Research, Industrial—Canada   3. Industry and education—Canada   I. Corporate-Higher Education Forum   II. Title

T177.C2C97 1985   507'.2071   C85-090264-9

Publishing Coordination by
  Ampersand Communications Services Inc.
Design and technical art by Artplus Limited
Typesetting by Linotext Inc.
Printed and bound in Canada by Les Editions Marquis Ltée.

CONTENTS

FOREWORD   1
PREFACE: MESSAGE FROM THE TASK FORCE   3
INTRODUCTION   9

1. BENEFITS   13
   −Benefits to Universities from
    Cooperative Research   14
   −Benefits to Corporations from
    Cooperative Research   17
   −Benefits to Canada from
    Cooperative Research   20
   −Bringing it all Together   21

2. BARRIERS AND HOW TO
   OVERCOME THEM   27
   −Near-Term Barriers to Increased
    Funding   27
   −Taking Advantage of Existing
    Opportunities   30
   −Creating the Right Opportunities
    for Cooperation   32
   −Three Basic Barriers   33
   −Four Motivational Barriers   37
   −Four Procedural Barriers   41
   −Researcher-to-Researcher
    Interchange   46

3. GOVERNMENT SPENDING
   PATTERNS   49
   −Direct Spending   49
   −Funding for Others' R&D
    Activities   52

**4. THE FORUM'S
   COMMITMENT**   *53*
   —Forum Initiatives   *53*
   —Forum Member Initiatives   *55*

SURVEY RESULTS AND ANALYSES
   A. Corporate R&D Expenditure
       Patterns   *61*
   B. External Funding Patterns for
       University R&D   *76*
   C. Membership of Boards by
       Occupation   *86*

APPENDICES
   A. List of Interviewees   *89*
       — Corporate Leaders   *89*
       — University Leaders   *91*
       — University Researchers   *92*
       — Others   *93*
   B. Members of the Forum
       1984-1985   *94*
   C. Selected Bibliography   *97*

FOREWORD

In the fall of 1984, the Corporate-Higher Education Forum published its first major study *Partnership for Growth: Corporate-University Cooperation in Canada.* As a result of that research project, the Executive Committee established a Task Force of members to examine in more detail one of the issues identified for further action: the research and development required for the innovations that are expected to play such a significant role in ensuring the competitiveness of Canadian industry in coming years.

Spending Smarter is a result of that work. The report was presented to the Third Annual Meeting of the Forum in May 1985 where it was overwhelmingly endorsed by the membership for publication.

We believe its findings and recommendations will be of interest to you, and we hope, to the country as a whole.

Chairman

Deputy Chairman

LLOYD I. BARBER
President and
Vice-Chancellor
University of Regina

ALLAN R. TAYLOR
President and
Chief Operating Officer
The Royal Bank of Canada

PREFACE:
MESSAGE FROM
THE TASK FORCE

The picture of Canadian research and development investment patterns that emerged in this project has convinced us that improved cooperation between universities and corporations represents a genuine and substantial opportunity for Canada to deploy its research and development (R&D) resources more effectively and that this opportunity should be exploited aggressively. Since there is abundant evidence that mere admonition and force of argument are almost always insufficient to convince the skeptical, Forum members are committing themselves to lead by example.

Universities and corporations alike believe that cooperative R&D can offer substantial benefits in a variety of forms. Universities recognize that such cooperation can yield not only additional research resources but also new intellectual challenges which can result in society-wide benefits through the application of research. These add up to a more exciting and challenging environment for teachers and students which in turn leads ultimately to better educational programs.

Corporations recognize that better educational programs mean better graduates, leading in turn to greater competitiveness, both within Canada and globally. They also recognize that universities are an excellent and convenient source of technological expertise, which they either cannot afford to develop in-house or cannot justify as a permanent department.

Canada's economy also benefits substantially in that university R&D is a key source of the technological advances that protect our existing industries—challenged as they are by cheap labour and other resources in developing countries—while creating new jobs in the new industries such technological advances spawn. Outstanding examples of job-creation arising from technological achievement in major universities and corporations exist today in the United States and the United Kingdom. In Canada we are only beginning to reap such benefits; Kanata is, perhaps, our leading example.

All these benefits lead us to believe that cooperative R&D offers a significant opportunity to improve Canada's sub-standard performance in the worldwide R&D stakes. (Canada's R&D spending has stalled at about 1.5 percent of gross domestic product—consistently below the levels in other developed countries.) Cooperative R&D also offers an opportunity to overcome, at least in part, the serious shortcomings in government research spending (which consumes a disproportionately large share of Canadian R&D dollars). Although government funded research has resulted in some technological advances, we found that many believe government R&D spending has contributed little to the advancement of Canada's economic competitiveness, either because of poor project selection or because of poor transfer of results into the commercial arena.

Despite perceptions of the important benefits which are available through cooperative R&D, activity is limited. Our research confirms the view that there are two major barriers; one cultural, the other logistical. By "cultural barrier" we mean the differences between the academic and corporate communities in terms of R&D goals, ways of doing things, attitudes toward time and budgets, and definitions of success. The "logistical barrier" relates to the practical difficulties researchers in both communities encounter in identifying and communicating with their counterparts to initiate cooperative activity.

On a more positive note, we found cooperative R&D being conducted to the satisfaction of both university and corporate participants. Two conditions appear to be necessary if such healthy cooperation is to continue to flourish and grow; and these are the two main messages of our report. *First*, leaders on both sides must create a more supportive environment, within which it is easy to deal with cultural or institutional differences. *Second*, organizations must invest the time and money to get researchers talking to researchers. Talking leads to specific project opportunities—and that is the payoff.

There is growing evidence that the climate is right for cooperative R&D to flourish. A consensus is emerging that there will be a tilt back toward basic research—the forte of the university—as corporations recognize the limitations inherent simply in seeking further refinements of existing technologies. At the same time, there is a growing recognition among academics that working with corporations does not necessarily imply an erosion of independence and integrity; even in the most intensely active cooperative relationships, contract work accounts for only a small percentage of a university's overall research budget.

We do not mean to play down organizational barriers. Some are so deeply entrenched, with solutions so radical to an organization's culture, that *only* leadership intervention will change things. Motivating researchers on both sides would be a beginning. At present, cooperative R&D is not likely to do much to enhance the career of a researcher on either side. Basic changes in evaluation systems are necessary to remove this barrier.

Spending Smarter builds substantially on the foundations laid by *Partnership for Growth* and other reports. In part, this report achieves our purpose to expand upon those studies (rather than simply to echo them) by drawing on additional data collected specifically for this project; this material has allowed us to gain insights which were not previously held. This report also achieves our purpose by identifying more precisely the nature of the fundamental cultural barriers that keep cooperative R&D from thriving in Canada, and proposing specific ways to begin dismantling these barriers. And, finally, this report achieves our purpose by encouraging Canadian governments to act as a source not only of money but also of ideas for both corporations and universities.

5

Listening to and synthesizing the perceptions and experiences of leaders in both the academic and corporate communities convinced us that we—corporations and universities together—must broaden our assault on the barriers to cooperative research by combining the power of researcher-to-researcher contact from the bottom up with improvement of the environment from the top down. In developing our detailed and specific remedies, we on the Task Force also built our own confidence in cooperative R&D itself.

Because one cannot learn to swim merely by reading a manual, our final chapter describes some concrete action to which Forum members have committed themselves. We ask others likewise to commit—if not to go further into the water, at least to get their feet wet.

J.V. RAYMOND CYR
Chairman
Forum Task Force

Members of the Task Force

Chairman: J.V. RAYMOND CYR
Chairman and Chief Executive Officer
Bell Canada

Members: ALEXANDER CURRAN
President
SED Systems Inc.

MYER HOROWITZ
President and Vice-Chancellor
University of Alberta

DAVID MCCAMUS
President and Chief Executive Officer
Xerox Canada Inc.

DONALD K. MCIVOR
Chairman and Chief Executive Officer
Imperial Oil Limited

ARNOLD NAIMARK
President and Vice-Chancellor
University of Manitoba

DOUGLAS WRIGHT
President and Vice-Chancellor
University of Waterloo

Project Director: DONALD ASSAFF
Director of University Liaison
Bell Canada

7

INTRODUCTION

In early 1984, after reviewing *Partnership for Growth*, its first study of university-corporate relationships, the Corporate-Higher Education Forum (the Forum) decided to pursue the issue of research and development, a top priority of the Executive Committee:

> [*A key*] *issue is the research and development required for the innovations that are expected to play such a significant role in ensuring the competitiveness of Canadian industry. What do members of the Forum consider to be the main impediments to a rapid increase in both the volume and the quality of the R&D effort in Canada and to its effective transmittal from the laboratory to the marketplace? Also, what roles can corporations and universities play in upgrading that effort over time?**

In mid-1984, the Forum established a Research and Development Task Force, consisting of four representatives from the private sector and three from universities across Canada. The Task Force accepted a mandate to examine the opportunities for and the impediments to furthering corporate-university cooperation in Canadian research and development in engineering and in the natural, medical, and applied sciences. (This selectivity does not imply that there are no opportunities for cooperative research in the humanities and social sciences or that these disciplines are less important than the so-called "hard" or technological sciences. The Forum simply bit off only as much as it thought it could chew at one time.)

---

*From the letter of transmittal from the Executive Committee.

9

The Task Force pursued its mandate in two parallel ways. Recognizing the Forum's distinctive capability in "searching out areas of agreement [between the corporate and university communities] and sharing the insights that come from a different perspective,"* it focused primarily on interviewing leaders of universities and corporations who are members of the Forum but also other prominent members of both communities. In addition, the Task Force undertook broad-ranging research and conducted extensive supplementary interviews.

Leadership interviews lasting up to 2 hours were conducted with the presidents of 10 universities and the chief executive officers, or their designates, of 25 major corporations. The perceptions of these leaders form the core of this report. It is important that readers note that none of those interviewed shared all the perceptions we encountered. In summarizing perceptions, the Task Force sought to make the clearest, most forceful statement on a subject possible. In some cases, therefore, our statement is more emphatic than the views held by some of the interviewees.

The extensive field work and research activity included:
- Surveys of corporate support of university R&D activities, involving 49 corporations and 14 universities—the first time such a comprehensive body of data has been assembled on this subject in Canada.
- Interviews with 20 professors to provide a practitioner's-eye view.
- Telephone and personal interviews with over 100 other respected authorities in Canada and abroad who are involved either directly in cooperative R&D themselves or indirectly as observers.
- Reviews of reports and other works published worldwide which address the effective commercial application of university R&D.
- Analyses of Canadian and other data on R&D spending, which is available publicly.

The purpose of this work was to provide a context in which to evaluate the observations our interviewees shared with us, to identify the magnitude of oppor-

---

*From the letter of transmittal from the Executive Committee.

tunities and problems, and to provide an international perspective on the subject.

Because of the limitations of a sample of even 35 leaders, the Task Force cannot comment definitively on several important sectors of our economy—such as agriculture, forestry, and the fishing industry. Clearly, these sectors are as important to Canada's economic well-being as are those we chose to study, especially since Canada is recognized as a technological leader in these sectors. Nonetheless, we are confident our findings apply equally to them.

A project team consisting of senior staff representatives from the Task Force members' organizations carried out day-to-day activities, from defining the issues through conducting the interviews and preparing this report. In addition, the Canadian practice of McKinsey & Company, the international management consulting firm, contributed its efforts as a public service—assisting in the interviews, designing and carrying out the statistical analysis, and helping to structure and write this report.

1

BENEFITS

This chapter examines the nature of the benefits which are to be derived from cooperative interaction by universities, corporations and Canadian society. *Universities* benefit at the individual researcher level as well as at the leadership or policy-making level. *Corporations* benefit whether they are large or small and whether or not they are resource- or technology-based. *Canadian society* benefits at large. Figure 1 summarizes these constituency-by-constituency benefits.

Again, it is important to note here that although our study does not encompass the entire scope of the Canadian economy, we believe the observations reported in this chapter apply virtually across the economic board.

Figure 1 Benefits From Interaction

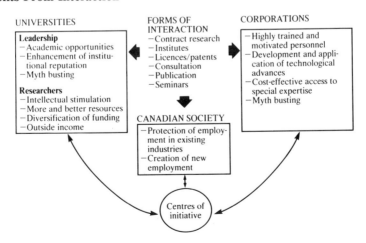

Benefits to Universities from Cooperative Research

If universities can be persuaded that it is smart to increase their emphasis on corporate-sponsored research and development, significant benefits—tangible and intangible—will result at both the leadership and the individual researcher levels.*

UNIVERSITY LEADERSHIP

Improving the levels of university-corporate cooperation will pay off handsomely in helping university leadership meet its responsibilities to provide its faculty and students with a broad and stimulating range of intellectual challenges and to build the institution's overall reputation.

Academic Opportunities. Cooperative research extends the range of intellectual challenges a university can offer teachers and students, and can enable a university to acquire a wider variety of physical resources than might otherwise be possible.

Enhancement of Institutional Reputation. A university's reputation will be enhanced as it achieves prominence as a place where meaningful, useful research is conducted, and as an institution which has the confidence of the business sector.

An earned reputation for having a sustainable research program with adequate facilities and brainpower is vital to an institution's ability to *attract and retain distinguished faculty* and to *recruit and place students*. A good researcher will almost certainly be more attracted to an institution that offers a broad range of research options and facilities and that can boast of students who are highly qualified, motivated and employable, than to one with a narrow range of options.

For its part, a corporation is more likely to hire a student who has participated in a joint project, who has hands-on familiarity with the industry, whose

*These are categories of convenience only and are in no way intended to suggest that benefits are important only to administrators and researchers.

"Primary benefits to university partners are an increased breadth of understanding through exposure to real-world problems, and enhancement of the university reputation."
CORPORATE CEO

"Through cooperation with industry, our university has made significant contributions and has acquired new knowledge to increase our intellectual inventory."
UNIVERSITY PRESIDENT

"A rewarding experience from the technology transfer—seeing their ideas used enhanced opportunities for student placement."
CORPORATE CEO

"Students are more employable—even in pure physics."
PROFESSOR

"Relevant material really makes my course come alive. The majority of my undergrad students are interested in practical applications."
PROFESSOR

"Our current testing machines define state of the art and are the fastest in the world–perhaps four or five times faster than NASA's."
PROFESSOR

"Dealing regularly and on a fairly intimate basis with industry is indispensible to our ability to remain vital. It's a good test of the relevance of what we teach."
DEAN OF ENGINEERING

"I might look to universities for research if staff there had experience in solving industrial problems."
CORPORATE CEO

"The professors were scientifically challenged."
CORPORATE CEO

"Many of our researchers work with industry because it enhances their research. There is room for a balance of directed research and contemplative basic research."
UNIVERSITY PRESIDENT

"It provides a parallel increase in breadth of their views and interests."
CORPORATE CEO

abilities are already proven, and who is conversant with that company's culture and current projects even before joining. In turn, the enhanced marketability of its degree should make it easier for a university to attract students with superior promise. A good illustration is one university whose faculty and students stand out consistently in competitions sponsored by a major oil company; as a direct result, its graduates are eagerly sought by Canadian auto manufacturers.

Mythbusting: The University's Side of the Coin. When the two communities get to know one another more intimately, one of the most desirable consequences will be the dismantling of false and negative notions each has about the other. As we discuss in more detail in the next chapter, stereotypes and reflexive preconceptions are involved to a notable degree in most of the barriers to increased cooperative research. Reducing if not eliminating them will substantially advance the Forum's overriding objective and the recommendations of the authors of this report.

Perhaps the chief stereotype to be attacked is the misguided notion that the individuals who constitute universities (administrators, faculty and students) dwell in ivory towers, spending the few hours they work in a blissful attempt to increase their isolation from the vulgar outside world.

We are convinced that this is an instance when more familiarity will breed respect.

RESEARCHERS
At least four benefits accrue to the university researcher from increased university-corporate cooperation: intellectual stimulation, better research resources, increased flexibility from diversifying the sources of funds, and the potential for additional income.

Intellectual Stimulation. Corporate research is a fruitful source of challenging problems. Some professors interviewed even suggested that it enhances the quality of contemplative research by suggesting new avenues for later independent exploration that might otherwise not have come to mind. Corporate research also builds awareness of goings-on in the

"I found that there are very important scientific questions that industry had to deal with that let me make a real contribution to chemistry."
PROFESSOR

"Contact and interaction with universities broadens the views and interests of internal researchers."
CORPORATE CEO

"Interaction with industry is crucial to understanding the direction of technological advancement. It helps to stay abreast of the rapidly changing environment."
PROFESSOR

"A practical and obvious benefit is the availability of more diverse resources."
UNIVERSITY PRESIDENT

"State-of-the-art equipment is critical to our research. Industry has helped us by giving or lending us equipment that would otherwise have been too expensive."
PROFESSOR

"Sponsored research provides benefits from equipment donations."
UNIVERSITY PRESIDENT

"With industry dollars [as a supplement to other R&D funds] I can hire more grads, do more research and publish a lot more."
PROFESSOR

corporate world. Activities that put researchers in contact with other researchers whom they might otherwise not encounter professionally are valuable. It is also exhilarating to see the actual application of one's own research.

More and Better Resources. In some disciplines, such as engineering and chemistry, sponsored research provides new equipment for the university researcher that might not otherwise be available. In addition, corporate contracts provide the wherewithal to build high-calibre research teams that are capable of making fundamental contributions to the advancement of knowledge.

Occasionally, a corporate-sponsored project generates more income than it spends. Frequently, the resulting surplus constitutes a fund the department or research team can use at its own discretion to support other research programs which university, government, and other corporate funds do not cover.

Diversification of Funding. The nature of the co-operative R&D dollar frequently makes it more attractive to the university researcher than an incremental Natural Sciences and Engineering Research Council (NSERC) or internal R&D dollar. Not only can corporate-sponsored research provide individual researchers with better equipment and human resources than might otherwise be available to them under university funding, but it also provides diversification of funding. This can lead to more security in funding because several sources reduce the risk that a cutoff (for whatever reason) in one will devastate an entire program. Furthermore, university and NSERC grants typically carry rigid spending restrictions and cut-off dates, which impose *a priori* limits on research flexibility. Corporate contracts, on the other hand, are usually defined by objectives. Corporate-research budgets and timetables, accordingly, derive from the nature of the project, and are less inclined to limit it.

Outside Income. University-corporate cooperation creates the real possibility that a researcher can

"I have gained financially from my research. Currently I am an equity holder and director of a company that I founded. I'm not alone; a colleague of mine recently sold a patent for more than $100,000."
PROFESSOR

"I think more and more professors are becoming aware of the market potential of their research. They are also discovering that they have talents that they can sell. I conduct contract research and have a modest consulting practice."
PROFESSOR

"Motivation in engaging in cooperative programs is to identify good students for potential employees."
CORPORATE CEO

"Universities provide results from some very adventurous science such as the application of biotechnology to processes in the pulp and paper industry."
UNIVERSITY PRESIDENT

". . . a major opportunity to identify the best students in universities."
CORPORATE CEO

increase his personal income. Outside consulting and contracts enable professors to supplement their academic salaries. Moreover, researchers may receive royalties or one-time payments for discoveries, although this category of income is much less predictable and immediate than income from consulting.

Benefits to Corporations from Cooperative Research

The corporate sector benefits from cooperative research in at least four important ways by: improving the training and motivation of future employees, developing (or acquiring) and applying new technologies, gaining cost-effective access to research expertise in unfamiliar fields, and improving the understanding of business in the academic world.

The first three of these corporate benefits will be particularly important as Canada's corporations feel the chill of increased international competition and turn to technology for their revitalization (as we believe is already beginning to happen). Our resource-based industries are already threatened by new, low-cost off-shore competition based on cheap labor and low-cost raw materials, often subsidized, at least indirectly, by governments seeking industrial development and export markets.

New technology will be the basis of the productivity breakthroughs many vulnerable Canadian companies need. For example, executives from two major oil companies interviewed agree that further development of Canada's oil sands depends on a breakthrough in extraction or upgrading technologies to permit better recovery in existing operations or profitable recovery from reserves that cannot now be exploited economically. Also, although Canada's manufacturing industries have suffered, the installation of IBM's new metallized ceramic substrates factory in Quebec proves that the most advanced manufacturing technologies can be established here against worldwide competition. Research which draws on the expertise in Canada's universities can provide part of the technological drive needed to establish these new manufacturing industries.

"As our interests expand to include the development of products in areas with which we are less experienced, we are monitoring research at universities with the goal of applying these results by integrating them into our systems."
CORPORATE CEO

"Just learning is important. If both the company and the university are not learning something new from the research, interest flags."
CORPORATE CEO

"We saw an improvement in the training of students hired from a local college whose data processing professors worked with our company during the summer. The professors solved some of our problems, too."
CORPORATE CEO

"If you don't do research in the university, the quality of education goes down."
CORPORATE CEO

"Graduates are the most important vehicle for transferring innovation from universities to corporations."
CORPORATE CEO

Highly Trained and Motivated Personnel. Cooperative R&D improves the quality and the relevance— that is, the applicability and corporate usefulness— of the student's academic experience. In fact, this is the benefit the corporate leaders interviewed mentioned most consistently, and the one almost unanimously acknowledged as the most important goal of their existing cooperative R&D efforts.

If universities have better facilities and more highly motivated teachers, the quality of instruction should improve. Students, for the most part, are more interested in working on projects that have real-life application and which provide them with genuine career opportunities than they are in working on primarily theoretical studies. Students who are intensely interested in their work and highly motivated also tend to inspire the faculty.

In addition, projects jointly undertaken enable corporations to get to know students and thus improve their employment screening processes. Students who have worked on problems with practical applications are more readily assimilated into the corporate work force, providing value to employers more quickly. As an example of collaboration, the University of Quebec has located part of its engineering school at a Bell-Northern Research lab facility, where students and professors work on real-life Bell product and service research challenges.

Development and Application Of Technological Advances. Corporations benefit from technological advances which improve internal *production methods* by reducing costs or enhancing quality, and which create new or improved *products or services* by providing superior value or lower prices for customers. Such technological advances may be the result of simple improvements to existing technologies. They may be innovative applications of existing technologies drawn from elsewhere, or they may involve the creation and application of wholly new technologies. In general, corporate R&D is well positioned to develop and apply incremental *changes in existing technologies*. For example, the yield from a catalyst may be improved by continuously adjusting operating conditions throughout the catalyst's life cycle.

18

"We participate with universities because it provides the corporation with a window on threats and opportunities."
CORPORATE CEO

The *new application of existing technologies* is an area in which cooperative R&D can bring substantial benefits because a corporation's own R&D efforts in foreign technologies tend to be exploratory and therefore unfocused. Universities often offer an ideal source of instant expertise. A good illustration is the adaptation of optical disk technology to computer information storage.

In the *creation and application of wholly new technologies*, universities offer corporations the opportunity to create wide "windows" on a range of new possibilities generated by basic research without having to commit resources in any specific scientific direction until technical uncertainties are minimal. These "windows" reduce the risk that a corporation will be blind-sided by a new technology, as were the makers of vacuum tubes by transistor technology, the makers of tire cord by the change from cotton to rayon to polyester, and medieval manuscript-illuminators by movable type. "Windows" require extensive and strong linkages with the universities, but not necessarily much cooperative R&D during the initial stages. Increased cooperation follows naturally as a new technology shows signs of great promise.

"Corporations benefit from low-cost labour in the form of graduate students."
CORPORATE CEO

"We used two professors who were specialists in their fields—they did in a year what we probably couldn't have done at all."
CORPORATE CEO

"We see universities as having extremely good talent and being relatively inexpensive."
CORPORATE CEO

Cost-Effective Access To Special Expertise. In both new technology development and the new application of existing technologies, universities offer corporations the important benefit of being relatively cost-effective places to gain access to expertise. It is unnecessary for a corporation to build teams or support them beyond their useful limits if the technology turns sour. A separate, although related, area in which universities have important cost advantages is in peripheral technologies, for which a corporation may only have limited need or a brand-new opportunity, for example, an oil company's need for coastal engineering expertise.

Mythbusting: The Corporation's Side of the Coin. As a general rule, when people are given a choice between the unknown and the familiar, they almost always choose the latter. Students who have not had direct contact with the world of business are often skeptical of it; a few are even openly hostile. To the extent that improved university-corporate cooperation enables students to understand the business world, it will inevitably break down some of the mythical barriers that misunderstanding erects. Familiarity leads to understanding which, in turn, can translate into good will. Several executives interviewed said they consider the simple matter of having the names of their companies mentioned favourably on campus to be an important goal of their cooperative research programs.

Benefits to Canada from Cooperative Research

Increased cooperation is likely to lead to more discoveries that will protect Canadian employment in existing industries and create new employment in new industries.

PROTECTING EMPLOYMENT IN EXISTING INDUSTRIES

In Canada's basic industries, it is almost inevitable that jobs will continue to be lost; the only question is how many. The impact of research—whether conducted by corporations, universities, government agencies, or any combination—will be to preserve as many Canadian jobs as possible over the long haul. It will also mitigate against the risk that entire sectors of the Canadian economy may disappear because of a failure to grasp technological opportunity. The challenge currently facing Canada's automobile industry from offshore producers who threaten to overwhelm the domestic market, thanks to technologically-derived lower costs, is one important example.

CREATING NEW EMPLOYMENT

Over the past decade, most new employment in Canada (and elsewhere) has been generated by small companies. Companies of 50 or fewer people provided about 70 percent of Canadian private-sector job growth from 1975 to 1980. As we look into the 1990s, most growth is projected in the information industries or is based on new technologies. The practical consequence of those forecasts is that Canadians should look to new companies as well as to the reinvigoration of entrepreneurship in existing enterprises (fashionably known as intrapreneurship) for new employment.

The Impact of New Ideas. New ideas create new jobs in many ways: first, for researchers and their assistants; second, in new companies formed to exploit those ideas; and third, in supporting companies formed to meet the needs of the new high-tech spin-offs. Every developer of software programs, for example, needs not only its presiding technical geniuses, but also business managers, marketing managers, and salespeople. A community of high tech spin-offs requires supporting service companies, from venture capitalists to fast-food restaurants.

Entrepreneurship in Mature Companies. Even when they succeed in maintaining the competitive edge of their core businesses, large corporations often still face a frustrating lack of growth opportunities. New technologies can provide new opportunities that are unavailable in the old. Domestic examples include Canadian Pacific, which expanded beyond rail transportation into air transportation; Ronalds-Federated, which added Alphatext electronic publishing to conventional printing; and Canada Wire and Cable, which is now involved in fibre optic cables that compete with its copper cables.

By now the reader will have anticipated our conclusion: that universities are a seedbed of new ideas which, when meshed with a corporate will to expand, have the potential to generate exciting new enterprises even within large corporations.

Bringing it all Together

High-tech communities and research parks illustrate best, and most visibly, how cooperative research advances the objectives of universities and corporations while creating new employment and protecting old jobs. Outstanding examples are Route 128 (Massa-

"I would be very receptive to a university wishing to take the initiative in developing new technologies that may be central to creating new jobs in existing companies."
CORPORATE CEO

"Universities have been used as tools of social development in this country. Now we've got to start using them as tools of economic development. And that means concentrating research and teaching expertise to create centres of excellence to benefit our economy."
CORPORATE CEO

chusetts) and Silicon Valley (California), which are renowned throughout the world. Flourishing newcomers are located in Cambridge, England (the Cambridge Phenomenon), and in North Carolina (Research Triangle Park). The Kanata region, near Ottawa, is probably Canada's leading example. We call these centres of technology-driven development "Centres of Initiative" to highlight their creation by multiple players and multiple factors. Figure 2 sets out the five key factors which our research convinced us are required if a Centre of Initiative is to flourish (see page 24-25).

(see page 24-25).

1. First and most important, success requires at least one champion who has a strong personal commitment—almost to the point of obsession—to ensure that something happens. The United States and Cambridge experiences indicate this champion is rarely, if ever, government.* Fred Terman, Dean of Engineering at Stanford, and John Bradfield, Senior Bursar of Trinity College, Cambridge, are acknowledged to have been the decisive champions. In Kanata, Alex Lester of Bell and Michael Cowpland of the Mitel Corporation may have played this role (although less deliberately than in the other instances we observed).

2. The second important criterion is the presence of at least one university with: a) an outstanding academic reputation; b) established capabilities in applied sciences and engineering; and c) a track record of active support for the corporate world. Although it is not necessary that a university play an activist role in developing a science park, U.S. and British experiences demonstrate that the very minimum requirement is that the university must be supportive. Cambridge provides a good illustration: the university acknowledges the right of its professors to take part in outside research activities not directly related to university teaching or research.

*Research Triangle Park is the notable exception to this observation. Of 31 research parks under development in the United States at present, few, if any, were initiated by any level of government.

"Current existing funding mechanisms should be reinforced and used to create centres of excellence".
CORPORATE CEO

"The key is research parks in which skills must be brought to bear if technologically-based professors are to succeed in commercializing their work."
CORPORATE CEO

3. Proximity of a major corporate or government R&D facility is a third condition that fosters development of centres of initiative. In many instances, this local facility has supported the science park by training the technical staff and by becoming the initial customer for some of the products and services produced by start-up companies. In California for example, the aerospace industry represented the key initial market for the early participants in the Stanford Industrial Park. Likewise, some of the success of Kanata can be attributed to the cooperation of the nearby National Research Council and Bell-Northern Research laboratories.

4. Venture capital must be available. Our interviews consistently identified the difficulty of finding appropriate venture capital to support high-technology initiatives as a major problem in Canada. Many stated that to the extent that financing is available here, it often comes from U.S. sources.

5. The physical environment—specifically, the conditions which attract scientists and their families on a personal level—is the fifth key factor. While some researchers are unquestionably motivated primarily by the intellectual challenge and career opportunities associated with working in a highly-charged creative atmosphere, there is no doubt it helps to have in place the infrastructure which makes the choice easy for them. Where climate is a hindrance, other "quality-of-life" considerations such as culture, affordable housing, calibre of public school systems, favourable tax climate, and general ambience must be especially promoted—and safeguarded.

Figure 2   Centres of Initiative

	Cambridge, England	Massachusetts – Route 128	North Carolina – Research Triangle Park	Silicon Valley – Stanford Industrial Park
Indicators of Growth	–Since 1960, the number of high-tech firms in the area has grown from 30 to 322 –Population growth from 1960 to 1980 increased by 28% or 1.8 million –Much of the job creation is in non-high-tech firms	–75,000 high technology added to the work force between 1975 and 1980 –In 1970 one-third of all manufacturing employment was in high-tech –up 30% since 1975	–20,000 employees in RTP from zero in 1960 –Population of Raleigh has doubled –41 companies in the Park	–In agricultural area in 1940 with a population of 175,000; by 1980 had grown to 1.25 million
Key Success Factors 1. One or more strong champions or leaders	–John Bradfield – Bursar of Trinity College, Cambridge –Matthew Bullock – Barclays Bank Manager	–None immediately evident although the venture capital firm of American Research and Development is frequently credited with having provided initial stimulus	–Luther Hodges – Governor of North Carolina from 1953-61 and more recently Ned Huffman, the Administrator	–Fred Terman initiated the idea with Hewlett-Packard
2. One or more outstanding local universities –With recognized capabilities in applied sciences/engineering	–Cambridge has a strong applied sciences faculty and an engineering faculty that is applied in its approach	–MIT, Harvard, and Northeastern all have strong computer and engineering faculties: area includes 25 more institutions of higher education, most with science and engineering faculties and many with research-oriented hospitals	–Duke, North Carolina State, and the University of North Carolina are recognized as being among the best in the South	–Stanford has been transformed into a national institution as a result of the interaction with the business community
	–Not so much supportive as laissez faire (allowing professors to pursue outside interests)	–MIT graduates constitute the single most important source of entrepreneurs in the region	–All major schools in the area have special teaching centres to train technical staff	
–Supportive of the corporate world				—

3. Proximity to a major R&D facility (either corporate or government)	– The government-financed Medical Research Council Laboratory is located near Cambridge	– Arthur D. Little	– Federal Government Environmental Protection Agency	– Ready customer in the form of government aerospace industry
4. Availability of active financing	– Barclays Bank actively supported and financed new business in the area – particularly computer related	– Boston is a major centre of venture capital financing ranking fourth in the United States	– Although venture capital is available in Charlotte, much of the initial funding has come from state government or university sources	– Venture capital funding in San Francisco ranks second in the United States
5. Attractive local environment				
– Climate and countryside	– Attractive city—climate good by U.K. standards	– Despite New England climate, offers attractive countryside within easy commute	– Mild yet 4-season climate in attractive countryside of rolling hills	– Attractive West Coast climate
– Availability of housing	– Reasonable, especially in surrounding villages	– Good housing stock in and around Boston; ample availability from declining industries	– Attractive housing costs	—
– Supply of trained technicians	– Strong supply from university labs; few competing for opportunities	– Local universities supply 80% of technicians employed by Route 128 companies	– State community colleges have put in place tailored programs	– Availability of low-cost labour has resulted in emphasis on manufacturing
– Transportation	– Good connections to London (road/rail) and access to Stansted airport	– Good connections both within United States and to Europe to a lesser extent	– Good transportation from Raleigh	– Good transportation facilities
– Available commercial land	– Major constraint until the opening of the Science Park under the auspices of Trinity College	– Generally available	– RTP is built on 5,500 acres of strictly zoned land	– The initial park was 660 acres
– Tax environment	– Same as other U.K. locations	—	– Very favourable	—
– Cultural and recreational opportunities	– Cultural centre based on the university	– Boston is a major U.S. cultural centre	—	– San Francisco is a major cultural centre

In short, the benefits of cooperative research are potentially great. It would be an overstatement to say that unless Canada doubles or triples its emphasis on cooperative research (or tries to meet any arbitrary quota) the future of the economy will be in jeopardy. Similarly, it would be an overstatement to suggest that all, or even a large proportion, of the nation's R&D spending lends itself to cooperative arrangements. As Figure 3 shows, however, there are significant areas where university expertise and corporate needs *do* overlap.

It is clear to us, and we believe it is becoming increasingly clear to universities and corporations, that in these realms both may be able to achieve their goals with hitherto unexpected efficiency and ease via the cooperative route.

The next chapter addresses ways to do just that.

Figure 3   Research Profiles of Universities and Corporations 1984 Estimates

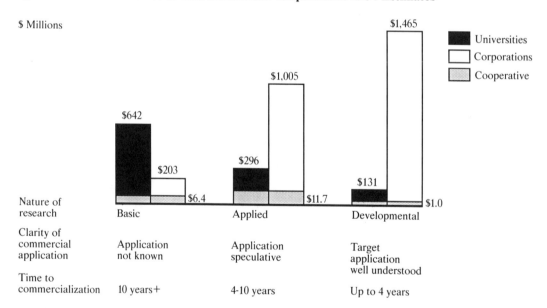

Source: Corporate profile is based on McKinsey analysis of Forum Corporate R&D Expenditure Survey of 49 leading performers responsible for more than 56 percent of 1984 corporate research spending as estimated by Statistics Canada. *University profile* is based on National Science Foundation estimates of United States college and university research profile applied to 1984 Canadian higher education research spending as estimated by Statistics Canada.

2

Barriers And How To Overcome Them

"There is a serious mis-distribution of funding in this country versus all other OECD nations. Canada, unlike other nations, has a strong tendency to do its research 'in-house' as opposed to contracting out . . ."
CORPORATE CEO

Despite a few signs of progress toward taking advantage of the opportunities described in the previous chapter, cooperative R&D in Canada accounts for a minuscule proportion of the total R&D activity—a total which is, in turn, anaemic compared with the R&D activity in other countries with which Canada competes. This chapter examines the barriers surrounding both phenomena—the comparative shortfall in R&D spending generally, and the comparative lack of emphasis on cooperation in terms of overall spending. Equally important, in this chapter we also address the ample opportunities we discovered for improving the quality of existing spending by removing the most harmful of those barriers.

Near-Term Barriers to Increased Funding

"The government doesn't realize the time frames involved in R&D and how the effect of cutting back today impacts the economy in the long term."
CORPORATE CEO

Numerous reports by organizations in both the public and the private sectors amply document Canada's comparatively low R&D investment levels. At less than 1.5 percent of gross domestic product, our spending levels have been consistently lower than the levels in other developed countries. Furthermore, our level of R&D investment has tended to remain flat (see Figure 4)—despite repeated and continuing exhortation to increase it.

Figure 4 **Proportion of Gross Domestic Product Devoted to R&D for Selected OECD Countries**

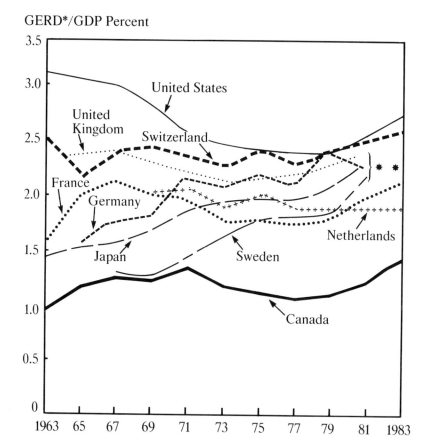

GERD*/GDP Percent

*Gross domestic expenditure on research and development, including Natural Sciences, Engineering, Social Sciences, and Humanities except for Sweden, and 1963-69 for Canada for which only NSE is reported.
**Data not available for 1983.

Source: Science and Technology Indicators Unit; OECD

Bringing Canada's R&D spending levels up at least to par with the rest of the developed world makes good national sense. But this report is no more likely to galvanize a national consensus to defer other

"Government R&D programs should be better managed—continually tested for relevance and success, and cancelled if not delivering on both counts."
CORPORATE CEO

priorities so as to enable diversion of significant new sums to research than the masses of earlier volumes on the subject. In any case, the notion that the problem can be solved simply by adopting an R&D spending target is naive. Even if the money did somehow materialize, it would be impossible, at least in the short term, to meet the demand for research talent that would result. According to a 1985 report prepared by the Natural Sciences and Engineering Research Council,* Canada's available domestic research talent projected through the rest of the 1980s will be adequate only with "no, or very slow, economic growth and no further significant increase in [the domestic R&D spending] target". The NSERC report also states that Canada cannot even meet the demand through immigration because there is a worldwide shortage of scientists in high-growth fields. Equally important, the report goes on to say that Canada runs "the real risk of losing to other countries the already limited talent being trained here" today.

Against the backdrop of the meagre emphasis Canada places on R&D overall, the cooperative aspect is even less impressive. Our survey of R&D spending for 1984 indicated that in that year, all businesses in Canada spent approximately $22.0 million on contractual research with North American universities; $19.1 million of that total was spent in Canada. (See Survey Results and Analyses A and B.) Canadian businesses also contributed an additional $30.4 million to university departments for scholarships, equipment, chairs, etc. These contributions were neither unrestricted contributions to the university general fund, nor were they project-related arrangements with the expectation of specific research results.**

Aggravating the shortage of dollars is the fact that, compared with most other countries, government in

---

Research Talent in the Natural Sciences and Engineering: Supply and Demand Projections to 1990—Background Study.

**These figures are extrapolated from our specific findings, which focused on 49 of the largest R&D spenders, accounting for 56 percent of the nation's overall non-government R&D spending. This sample spent $12.4 million on contract R&D research with North American universities in 1984, and directed an additional $17.1 million to departments for non-directed R&D.

"The examples of govern-
ment misapplication of R&D
time and money are legion.
Most of what they do is a
waste of time."
PROFESSOR

"With respect to R&D, government is a 'missionless'
institution which has neither
a focused commercial objective nor a more broadly
based knowledge-building
objective to drive research."
CORPORATE CEO

Canada is proportionately a much bigger player in R&D spending (see Figure 5). While there is general agreement that Canada's governments deliver impor-tant and useful services to private industry, chiefly in the area of testing, there is also virtually unanimous agreement in the rest of the research community (corporations and universities alike) that government in-house R&D is relatively ineffective in that programs are poorly chosen for purposes of economic develop-ment and results are badly disseminated. Govern-ment-performed research produces neither the direct economic benefit of corporate R&D nor the body of trained students created by universities.

Until overall spending can be increased and until the balance of government/university/corporate R&D can be shifted, Canada has a pressing need for the benefits of cooperative R&D.

Taking Advantage of Existing Opportunities

"Technical universities are
much more helpful to cor-
porations than science departments of undergraduate
universities because their
research has a greater applied content."
CORPORATE CEO

Even apart from the comparative lack of emphasis in Canada on R&D spending in general, corporations in Canada appear to be much less committed to co-operative research with universities than are their counterparts elsewhere. While there are no precise, reliable data on the matter, there is a consensus among the authorities we consulted in both the cor-porate and university communities that cooperative research represents less than one percent of all research spending by Canadian companies. Further-more, our observations in three respects lead us to conclude that cooperative R&D is much more widely undertaken in the countries with which Canada com-petes: the visibility of cooperative activity, the level of importance ascribed to it by national policy-makers, and the richness of discussion about such research in serious international periodicals.

"The technically centred
schools, such as Waterloo,
are fundamentally more
helpful than [broad-based]
universities."
CORPORATE CEO

As indifferent as Canadian business may be to the notion of contracting with universities to conduct corporate research, universities seem equally so. The business community perceives that comparatively

Figure 5   Gross Expenditures on R&D (GERD)   1981

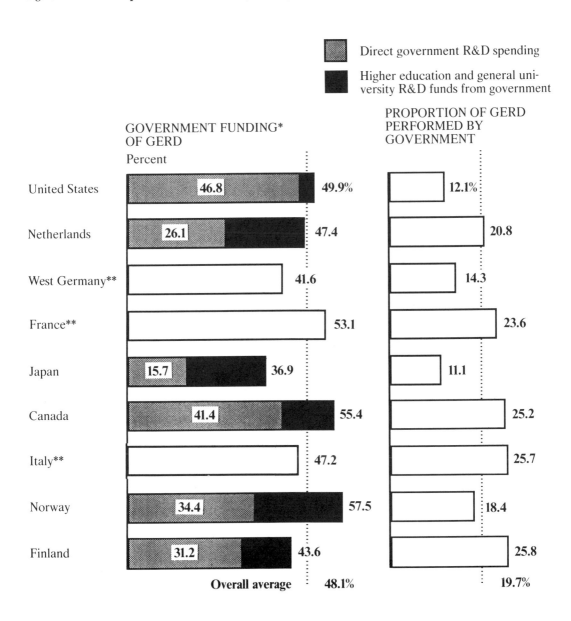

Direct government R&D spending

Higher education and general university R&D funds from government

GOVERNMENT FUNDING* OF GERD
Percent

PROPORTION OF GERD PERFORMED BY GOVERNMENT

	GOVERNMENT FUNDING* OF GERD	PROPORTION OF GERD PERFORMED BY GOVERNMENT
United States	46.8 / 49.9%	12.1%
Netherlands	26.1 / 47.4	20.8
West Germany**	41.6	14.3
France**	53.1	23.6
Japan	15.7 / 36.9	11.1
Canada	41.4 / 55.4	25.2
Italy**	47.2	25.7
Norway	34.4 / 57.5	18.4
Finland	31.2 / 43.6	25.8
Overall average	48.1%	19.7%

*Data may not be strictly comparable due to definitional differences of government funding especially with respect to treatment of general university and higher education funds.

**Separate data not available for direct government R&D spending and general R&D funds for universities and higher education.

Source: OECD/STIU Data Bank

31

few Canadian universities regard their fundamental mission as equipping students to work productively in the applied sciences in business upon graduation. The University of Waterloo (Ontario), l'Ecole Polytechnique (Quebec), and the Technical University of Nova Scotia are among the most notable exceptions. Canada has no Massachusetts Institute of Technology, no Cal Tech. Moreover, those with whom we talked seemed to sense that in Canada's broad-based universities, science and engineering faculties need to become more open and empathetic toward the business world.

Creating the Right Opportunities for Cooperation

Research and development is one way to achieve the organizational objectives of both the university and the corporation. In universities, the overriding objective is to increase understanding; in corporations, it is to improve efficiency or create new, desirable goods and services for society and hence create economic benefits for employees and shareholders.

The nature of research undertaken by each community differs in important ways. Universities focus typically on *basic* research—that is, on research most likely to expand knowledge generally, and thereby to enhance the researcher's reputation. The corporate world focuses on *applied* research—that is, on new products and processes that can be exploited commercially. University research tends to be more theoretical, curiosity-driven and less constrained to deliver specific, predetermined results within a specific period. It is conducted openly. Publication, in the broadest sense, is essential to professional recognition. It is also essential to stimulating discussions among researchers—grist for the mill of developing, testing, and clarifying ideas. Corporate research, in contrast, tends to be more practical, goal-oriented and subject to commercially driven deadlines. In a competitive environment it is also—necessarily—secretive.

It is not surprising, then, that the amount of cooperative R&D is small. Cooperative programs are

"The contrast in cultures is a major barrier."
UNIVERSITY PRESIDENT

"University cultures often devalue commercially oriented research."
CORPORATE CEO

"Universities lack a business perspective and we have limited experience in dealing with science—the result is communications barriers on both sides."
CORPORATE CEO

"Universities have a difference of urgency—they take much longer do things than we can tolerate."
CORPORATE CEO

"If you leave it to the scientists in each organization, their objectives and motives are the same. Letting them get to know each other is very important. This is what creates opportunities."
CORPORATE CEO

"Successful innovators make more effective use of outside technology and advice."
RESEARCHERS

appropriate only when the nature of a specific project is appealing and important in both communities. Our interviews suggest that some of the reluctance to engage in cooperative R&D today stems from disappointing experiences in the past. We believe this is due primarily to poor selection of cooperative projects on both sides.

A key to successful cooperative R&D is to get researchers talking with researchers. When researchers in a particular field identify and define a cooperative project, a common goal is created. The difficulties of bridging the two cultures can then be tackled. Researcher contact—researcher networking—creates the right opportunities. However, before corporations and universities can begin to create researcher networks, they have to create environments in which such networks will flourish.

First, three divisive issues must be addressed: the nature of appropriate research, confidentiality, and project management. Second, motivational barriers which inhibit cooperative action must be removed through increasing understanding between the two communities. A good starting point might be a review of membership on each others' boards (see Survey Results and Analyses C). Finally, unproductive policies and practices must be abandoned, so that researcher networking can flourish.

Three Basic Barriers

If the three fundamental issues that seem most often to divide universities and corporations into opposing factions can be resolved—the nature of research (that is, the balance between basic and applied), confidentiality (the need to publish versus the need to patent), and project management (attitudes toward objectives, budgets, and deadlines)—we believe the remaining barriers can be disposed of readily.

ISSUE:

Nature of the Research

CORPORATION: Research must focus on projects with a clearly definable impact on products or processes.

UNIVERSITY: Research should be driven by curiosity; it represents an opportunity to expand knowledge. Any project that is interesting or stimulating to the researcher is worthwhile.

If cooperative activities are to flourish, better selection of projects is necessary. Toward this end, *each* organization must:

- Identify research projects which will sustain Canadian industrial vitality (and thus employment).

- Screen projects carefully as to their nature—i.e., where does each project fit in the spectrum between basic and applied?

- Designate someone to be accountable for the independent review of projects that remain potentially viable—solely on the grounds of their merit—as cooperative activities.

One Forum member company finds it helpful to use a matrix (Figure 6) in evaluating and screening its basic R&D activities, with *knowledge* and *application* forming the axes. Today, that company increases the applied emphasis of its research activities successfully, without sacrificing knowledge-building. The objective for tomorrow is to maintain a sharp focus on application while increasing knowledge-building. The company that developed this device uses it to assess in-house activities as well as cooperative efforts.

Increased contact between industry and the university will create the opportunity to accomplish several objectives. First, today's basic research, which may begin by being low on both application and knowledge building, will become more focused and effective. Second, increased communication will result in improved applications content of the research dealing with problems of today. Third, over time, research activities will accommodate both greater knowledge-building *and* higher applications content. That is tomorrow's objective.

"Industry's orientation is toward solving short-term problems. They are not interested in long-term research."
UNIVERSITY PRESIDENT

"Our goal is to expand the boundaries of science. Our long-term focus tends to conflict with the short-term focus of industry."
UNIVERSITY PRESIDENT

Figure 6   Research Focus

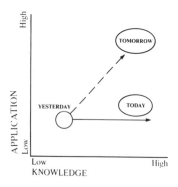

Source: Imperial Oil Limited

ISSUE: *Confidentiality*

CORPORATION: Technology-based competitive advantage demands secrecy (patent rights for product composition or process).

UNIVERSITY: The researcher's reputation, promotion and tenure demand highly visible, timely publication of research results—"publish or perish".

Together, universities and corporations must:

- Agree to exempt non-proprietary components of projects from non-disclosure agreements. Researchers, not only administrators, should help define "proprietary" elements on a case-by-case basis.

- Recognize and exploit long lead times for scholarly journals, and build this explicitly into formal agreements—i.e., cooperate with writing and with confidential peer review of prospectuses and drafts of articles under contractual commitment. This will ensure that research activities or results are not published or generally circulated (outside a specifically agreed-upon reading-and-review group) before a competitive advantage (such as patent protection) is secured.

- Agree on security of facilities and on limitations as to who can and cannot participate as part of a cooperative research contract.

For their part, universities can incorporate non-publishable results of research into their reward systems for tenure, promotion and salary review decisions. NSERC and some universities have already begun to do this by accepting patents as the equivalents of major research papers in their evaluation systems.

"It isn't just a matter of publication rights. The work is done in open labs. Anybody can come in and look. Students work on it, and then can get hired by our competitors."
CORPORATE CEO

"They want to publish—we want to capitalize on research we have funded. We tend to run into problems over patents and royalty rights."
CORPORATE CEO

"...and over involving postgraduates who need to write theses and publish."
UNIVERSITY PRESIDENT

"Some university projects you can divide into sensitive and non-sensitive areas, and then you need restrict publication only in the sensitive areas."
UNIVERSITY PRESIDENT

ISSUE:

Project Management (Objectives, Budgets, Deadlines)

"The notion of deadlines and schedules is a foreign one to most university researchers."
CORPORATE CEO

"University professors and adminstrators simply don't know what good project management is in a business."
CORPORATE CEO

"Universities want to analyze, quantify, and theorize before they act—they are not used to time pressure for a workable solution. They are always coming back for more money."
CORPORATE CEO

"Universities don't see the point of progress reports. They want to report at completion."
CORPORATE CEO

"Corporations want to work in short time frames and the university creates time pressure for results—it's difficult for us."
UNIVERSITY PRESIDENT

"[Corporations] spend time and money on frequent review meetings in the early stages of the project."
CORPORATE CEO

CORPORATION: Sound business practice demands tight control, but university professors seem unwilling or unable to exercise necessary discipline.

UNIVERSITY: Business is willing to allow dollar-chasing to stifle the valid role of academic activity: expansion of knowledge for knowledge's own sake.

These concerns can be reduced to comfortable tolerability through contract negotiations. With a commonly agreed-upon goal and meaningful rewards (intellectual, tangible, or both), these should become minor considerations as experience in managing them accumulates.

- Corporations should encourage university researchers to follow up on interesting digressions *after* objectives have been met—perhaps by including an incentive sum in the original budget for on-time/within-budget completion of the project.

- Universities must foster project-management skills—for instance, by designating a business-administration instructor or assistant to work with scientists in this respect.

- Corporations and universities should both be careful to focus their discussions on projects with budgets and deadlines which are not so tight that they fall outside the university's ability to manage. In other words, corporations must be candid about their expectations, and universities about whether a project can, in fact, be undertaken with a reasonable probability of success both substantively and logistically.

The next two sections address the motivational and the policy and procedural issues that must be resolved in order to create a supportive environment for cooperative R&D.

Four Motivational Barriers

Even after corporations and universities recognize and adjust to the differences between them, there are at least four insidious inhibitors which require strong signals from the top of the organization if they are to be handled satisfactorily.

ISSUE:

Wariness About the Real Nature of Cooperative Dealings

CORPORATION: Universities use research as a poorly disguised means of extracting money they intend to spend in their own way.

UNIVERSITY: Corporate money has strings attached, which inevitably compromise the independence and integrity of the university.

"University researchers have to change their attitude about corporate dollars— they are not dirty."
CORPORATE CEO

"I'm really concerned about professors working on commercial opportunities—they become secretive so readily. I'm afraid it will harm the quality of research done here."
UNIVERSITY PRESIDENT

"Industry must not be so domineering in its approach to universities. It must not appear to want to run the universities."
CORPORATE CEO

Both corporations and universities must learn that the objectives of the other are neither inherently more noble nor more base than their own. Their motives are, in fact, compatible. Each side should be candid in expressing the *quid pro quo* it expects from cooperation: for the *corporation*, commercially exploitable research findings that it cannot get as quickly, as economically or as readily (or all three) in any other way; for the *university*, challenges, resources, and professional achievement that its researchers cannot get as conveniently, if at all, in other ways.

ISSUE:

"Not Invented Here"

CORPORATION: Preference is for in-house research, sometimes even at the expense of cost effectiveness and speed.

UNIVERSITY: Ideas and objectives proposed outside the ivory tower are somehow less virtuous, valid or important than ideas generated internally.

"Lack of peer recognition for cooperative work—whether it's because it can't be discussed or because it's viewed as selling out—it's a real problem."
CORPORATE CEO

"Universities' approach to problem solving is uninhibited, whereas our people sometimes approach a problem with an inherent mindset that is hard to break."
CORPORATE CEO

"U.S. universities value cooperative research and this is reflected in their compensation programs—Canadian universities don't do this."
CORPORATE CEO

"Applications problems can lead to new exciting avenues of research—heart/lung machine damage to blood has resulted in quite new thinking about the surface structure of polymers."
UNIVERSITY PRESIDENT

"Commercial applications of value to mankind can and do excite professors who find a new kind of recognition and reward in beneficial application of their research—witness the expert on colloids who is now involved in the development of artificial lenses for the human eye."
UNIVERSITY PRESIDENT

It is not fiscally responsible or feasible for corporations to sustain technical capability in every area of potential relevance. Neither can universities responsibly suppose that they have a monopoly on the generation of all challenging, rewarding and interesting ideas, or that they do not need the additional resources cooperative research makes available.

- When they suspend preconceptions and actually undertake a cooperative project, researchers typically find that there is actually no merit in either point of view.

- Both corporate and academic leaders must take concrete steps to tear down reward systems which place a premium on the notion that the merit of a project proposal or the result of a project should be judged on any basis other than its own intrinsic worth. They must ensure that such counterproductive systems are replaced with reward structures that place a premium on cooperative efforts.

38

ISSUE:

Corporate Doubts about the Usefulness of University Expertise

"No Canadian university has the level of expertise in our technologies that we have in-house. We have to help them teach. They take our graduates."
CORPORATE CEO

"In some areas an outsider who doesn't know our systems, our plants, the processes we use today simply couldn't help without coming up a long and expensive learning curve."
CORPORATE CEO

"We don't know enough about university capabilities — we are not confident there are people out there able to help us."
CORPORATE CEO

"We never see a need to go to universities; our people think they are the best."
CORPORATE CEO

"We have found that research being done in universities is based on less understanding than that shared in our own labs."
CORPORATE CEO

Corporations frequently express doubts as to whether universities can really help them. This is particularly true among corporations in relatively mature technologies — technologies that have been applied commercially for many years. Opportunities for university researchers to help on corporate problems may indeed be limited if only core technologies are considered. Often corporate experience vastly exceeds the experience any university can bring to bear. But peripheral technologies (an oil company's need for coastal engineering expertise, for example) and "next" technologies (such as the carbon fibre tire cord that may replace polyester) are another matter. In cases such as these, universities can be the most cost-effective source of expert help.

Surprisingly, small fast-growing high-tech companies also express doubts as to whether universities can help them. Their reluctance seems to reflect a combination of "no time to look" and a desire to keep life-blood technical expertise in-house. To the extent that this attitude can be changed, it will probably require a strong marketing effort by universities of their areas of expertise. Some means of cataloguing company needs for expert R&D assistance would help universities make contact with both small and large companies. This proposal implies that there would be a matchmaker (the Forum, perhaps) with which a company requiring expertise could register; the matchmaker would identify the sources of relevant expertise.

ISSUE: *Talent Availability*

"Good people are busy and we find it difficult to get on their schedules."
CORPORATE CEO

CORPORATION: "The good researchers are all too busy."

UNIVERSITY: "I'm too busy."

"Good people tend to be too busy and are unable or unwilling to spend a great deal of time on any one project."
CORPORATE CEO

"Too busy" is often a euphemism for "not interested". If a proposed project offers more rewarding challenges than current research, time is likely to become available.

In universities, there is a sort of corollary to Parkinson's Law: *good* projects attract top-flight people who find the time to work on them. When universities and corporations see researchers consistently in demand to work on cooperative projects, this may be a signal that a Centre of Initiative is in the making. Leaders should encourage a champion to come forward.

"It is very tough to find the right person in the university who is both capable of doing the work and able to muster sufficient interest to sustain enthusiasm."
CORPORATE CEO

Four Procedural Barriers

There is, in addition, a set of policy or procedure-related obstacles that requires systematic attention. The removal of these obstacles will also be speeded up by direct researcher-to-researcher contact.

ISSUE: *Inadequate Marketing by Universities*

"We wouldn't know where to look for help among Canadian universities."
CORPORATE CEO

"Universities are not good at making their capabilities known—they have to do this better."
CORPORATE CEO

"Universities and businesses need to develop action plans to realize more transfer of information about their R&D activities."
UNIVERSITY PRESIDENT

"There is a real advantage to be gained from having a national directory of projects conducted at universities."
CORPORATE CEO

"Communications between us and universities are poor —the interface is not as good as it could be."
CORPORATE CEO

"The thing that could help us more is to have a way to find out what universities are doing."
CORPORATE CEO

CORPORATION: The corporation often cannot easily find out which universities or professors they should contact in order to discuss a possible project.

UNIVERSITY: It is undignified and potentially compromising to independence to pander to and solicit projects from a corporation by promising to achieve a predefined result.

Universities that are open to cooperative research must broadcast their interest throughout the corporate world, and can do so by:

- Designating a R&D liaison officer to disseminate information widely to corporations—perhaps by instituting a newsletter,

- Compiling, publishing, and distributing a comprehensive periodic index of researchers' areas of expertise,

- Freeing up researchers from certain non-teaching duties to work directly in corporate offices (e.g., allowing this to substitute for committee work).

If it is true that universities can do a better job of marketing their research expertise, it is equally true that corporations can do a better job of designating specific researchers or research managers to work with university marketing personnel, in effect, to be research purchasing agents.

Corporations and universities alike can share information several ways. For instance, they might:

- Make time available for non-project-related interchange among researchers, and reward participants for advancing the quality of relationships.

- Make explicit provision for membership on each others' research advisory boards/committees.

"U.S. universities have well-organized liaison programs and market their skills well. Canadian universities don't bother. As a result it's relatively hard to find Canadian expertise."
CORPORATE CEO

"Corporate groups should conduct detailed scanning of university capabilities."
CORPORATE CEO

"[We need] high-quality seminars where corporate researchers work on theory and case studies—not just theory-oriented lectures used as fund-raisers."
CORPORATE CEO

- Establish a new, prestigious (which probably means well-funded) annual award or other honour to acknowledge outstanding example(s) of individual research cooperation.

- Establish "windows" (managed, perhaps, by a third party such as the Forum) at universities with expertise in new or emerging technologies.

ISSUE: *Contract Complexity*

CORPORATION: University researchers want a virtual licence to do whatever they want and are reluctant to recognize that, in exchange for funds or other resources, a set of clearly defined expectations must be met.

"Both sides should have one or two experienced negotiators who are part of the team in every negotiation."
CORPORATE CEO/
UNIVERSITY PRESIDENT

UNIVERSITY: "They take a 2-page memorandum of understanding and toss it back at us as a 20-page contract. They want us to spend as much time telling them in detail what we intend to do as we spend actually doing it."

A standard, short-form model contract should be developed to avoid having to "reinvent the wheel" every time a cooperative project is contemplated. Negotiations would consist of agreeing on deviations from the norm. It makes a good deal of sense to us that the Forum should take the lead in developing such a model contract.

"Universities and corporations should create a standard contract, and negotiate deviations."
CORPORATE CEO/
UNIVERSITY PRESIDENT

"We have to learn how to approach each other."
CORPORATE CEO

Each party should designate an experienced negotiator of cooperative contracts to take part in the discussions. The substance of the negotiations should be conducted by scientists, however, not lawyers.

"The first few contracts with a university research team must be carefully selected to reduce the risk of failure, especially if the corporate culture emphasizes careful planning and studies before taking action. Risk may be minimized by scaling down the size and duration of the contract through phasing."
CORPORATE CEO

ISSUE: *Interdisciplinary Walls*

CORPORATION: "Whenever we have a problem that needs researchers from different departments—an interdisciplinary team—we have the greatest difficulty getting universities to respond."

UNIVERSITY: "Working on a project for another dean gets me nothing except problems—no recognition in my own department and distance from my own colleagues."

I deally, a university facilitator would help to identify the appropriate potential participants in various fields. For example, among leading universities in the United States, Stanford and MIT have little difficulty mobilizing multidisciplinary teams. Corporate researchers must also recognize, however, that they have a particular responsibility to motivate university researchers to undertake or to join a project, and that they will have to do this on a personal basis.

"It's very hard to get a university to put together a multidisciplinary team."
CORPORATE CEO

"Make a university liaison officer responsible for the multiple contacts needed initially."
CORPORATE CEO/
UNIVERSITY PRESIDENT

"Because of strong faculty or functional lines in the universities they are not able or willing to bring the right mix of science to problems —in contrast to, say, MIT."
CORPORATE CEO

ISSUE: *Geopolitics*

Both the university and corporate sectors recognize that distance (which is sometimes as much a psychological barrier as a physical reality) can impede cooperation. Even when a corporation recognizes the potential value of drawing upon university research expertise, travel time and cost, especially east-west, can be a crippling demotivator. But corporations also recognize the desirability of spreading their largesse more or less evenly across the geographical areas in which they operate.

The issue has, in our view, no structural solution. Corporations should cultivate nearby universities. To the extent that the cost of travel is a significant barrier, both universities and corporations can try to make adequate extra funds available. Both must recognize that north-south relationships with U.S. institutions or corporations may be more convenient and as productive as east-west relationships in Canada.

When things are equal, corporations should continue to disperse their R&D funds evenly. But when things are unequal, corporations should not—and universities must not expect them to—bypass unique or clearly outstanding university research capabilities because of geographical considerations or national boundaries.

"Although many Canadian companies recognize the need to spread their resources across the nation, those universities nearby always benefit most, if only because the chief executive officer is on the Board of Governors of the local institution."
UNIVERSITY PRESIDENT

"We will probably start building up some links—we'll concentrate on our local institutions so it will be easier to go and see them."
CORPORATE CEO

"The fact of the matter is that it's easier for us in Toronto to join forces with Toronto, or McMaster, or Waterloo than even with, say, Montreal. Working with the University of British Columbia is something we do because they've got what we want—actually the distance is a real nuisance."
CORPORATE CEO

"There is a political tendency to spread resources across the country. CAD/CAM multiple centres are a total misdistribution of funds. Canada can only afford one of these major centres if it is really to be at the leading edge."
CORPORATE CEO

Researcher-to-Researcher Interchange

The action suggested in the earlier sections of this chapter should remove existing impediments and barriers, real or perceived. That is, action that is directed at neutralizing *negative* considerations.

No less important, however, is *positive* action—action that will build and reinforce the benefits of corporate-university cooperation. For the most part, the two courses of action are quite independent of one another—but complementary.

The list that follows is illustrative and merely representative of the many kinds of action that can and should be taken. It is meant simply to provoke both the corporate and the university communities to find imaginative ways of keeping the interchange vital and ongoing.

- *Lecture series.* Appropriate university departments and corporate functional areas can initiate regular programs—lunches, for instance—to which researchers (not managers) from both sectors will be invited to discuss work under way.
- *Staff exchanges.* At least one program already exists in Canada under which university and corporate researchers exchange positions for a full year. Each continues to be paid by his permanent employer, but in all other respects each is expected to meet the requirements of the host institution.
- *Professional staff development.* Researchers should be aggressively encouraged (perhaps by incorporating this expectation into reward structures) to attend and actively participate in symposia, institutes, professional associations, conventions, etc.
- *R&D committee membership.* Corporations and universities each can formally designate one or more seats on their R&D planning committees to be filled by representatives from the other community.
- *Equipment.* On an ad-hoc basis, corporations and universities can share the cost of purchasing equipment that neither can afford or justify individually.
- *University outreach.* More Canadian universities should adopt programs similar to that of the Mas-

"There are no real differences in attitude between corporate and university researchers. Both are motivated by intrinsic interest and the advancement of their research programs."
UNIVERSITY PRESIDENT

"University researchers should spend sabbaticals in industry to learn about the kinds of problems we're tackling."
CORPORATE CEO

"University faculties which have industrial advisory committees are very successful."
CORPORATE CEO

"Bringing university professors in on sabbaticals can be a good idea."
CORPORATE CEO

"Companies should form consortia to sponsor university research where they share problems not central to their competitiveness—for example, in safety and environmental areas."
CORPORATE CEO

"We need ways of reducing the psychological distance between university researchers and corporations."
UNIVERSITY PRESIDENT

sachusetts Institute of Technology, under which individual professors accept responsibility for cultivating specific companies—that is, Professor X scans the environment (both internal and external, including journals) for intelligence and ideas that might, even remotely, be useful to Company Y. He regularly brings his Company Y counterpart up to date, either by means of a formal report or an informal get-together.

- *Funds facilitator.* Universities may be able profitably to hire an experienced professional who knows where the money is in corporations—in effect, a funds-finder who would monitor the external environment and suggest to a particular researcher that a particular company in an appropriate field may be ready to embark on a project of interest.

3

GOVERNMENT SPENDING PATTERNS

Although the Task Force did not work directly with government or its agencies, a number of recommendations for government action or investigation emerge naturally from our work. The Task Force believes that government should re-examine its policies and practices along two broad lines: *first*, its own direct spending on research and development; *second*, its tax and direct grant policies in support of research and development carried out elsewhere. While we believe the initiatives described in previous chapters will go a long way to improve the return Canada gets from its R&D dollar, there is no doubt that government, as a major player, is well positioned to improve significantly the effectiveness of Canada's overall R&D spending.

Direct Spending

Canadian governments are disproportionately large participants in research and development. We believe there are significant opportunities to improve the way in which that money is spent, and although this recommendation is hardly new, we believe another look at the issue is warranted. Two specific opportunities emerge as a result of our research and analysis.

"Government should get out of basic research by contracting out to industry and universities."
CORPORATE CEO

"Government should focus on enhancing university R&D, and on technology transfer into the market-place—not on doing the R&D itself."
CORPORATE CEO

"The Federal government's role should be taking the lead in encouraging others to do research and development."
CORPORATE CEO

"As a first step in improving the situation, the government should unwind its facilities and redeploy the funds to universities and corporations."
CORPORATE CEO

"Much of the research done in government never sees the light of day or it provides very little value."
CORPORATE CEO

SUBCONTRACT MORE, DO LESS IN-HOUSE

In an important 1983 talk and subsequent article on this subject, Roland W. Schmitt, head of the research-and-development division of the General Electric Company, described the ideal role of government involvement in R&D in a way with which nearly all our interviewees and the members of the Task Force agree. In this regard, he said, "The most important step that government can take is to ensure and strengthen the health of our university system—in both the performance of basic research and the training of research manpower. . . . Government has a crucial role to play in creating favourable conditions for commercial innovation, but not in actually producing those innovations."*

There is strong evidence both in Canada and elsewhere (principally the United States), to support Schmitt's view. In the United States, several studies of Defense Department spending have demonstrated convincingly that technological innovations are distributed much more widely through the economy and are more rapidly commercialized when subcontractors do the work.

It is generally agreed that government can often achieve its research objectives at less cost through subcontracting than it can by conducting the research in its own laboratories. This is a natural extension of our recommendation that corporations view universities as a source of R&D for those projects that do not require in-house expertise. We believe governments require little direct in-house research capability (except, perhaps, for defence research) and that virtually all other R&D could advantageously be subcontracted either to universities or to corporations.

It is important to note that we are hardly reaffirming the so-called "make-or-buy" R&D policy the Federal government inaugurated in 1972, which has, by all accounts, failed completely to achieve the reasonable objective of ensuring the flow of all potentially commercializable government-sponsored research findings into the private sector. The Economic Council

---

*"National R&D Policy: An Industrial Perspective," *Science*, June 15, 1984, pp. 1206—09.

"The top priority should be the modification of the role of NRC—which is too much an ivory tower. Its efforts should be dispersed geographically to help create centres of excellence."
CORPORATE CEO

of Canada concluded in 1982 that the make-or-buy directive had "not produced significant benefits to date" because, for the most part, the only federal agencies that bothered to comply with it were those "generally engaged in R&D with less commercial potential."*

We think it is probably a mistake simply to issue a policy directive (such as the make-or-buy edict) because it is too easy and too tempting for those affected to find loopholes or other ways to preserve the *status quo*. Here again, an incentive system— rewarding federal researchers and managers of research who promote effective interchange (financially, perhaps, in a way akin to royalties or, perhaps, in a way tied to career advancement)—might be an attractive option.

FIND MORE EFFECTIVE WAYS TO
COMMERCIALIZE RESULTS

Even when government declines to subcontract R&D activity, it remains important to ensure that government research results find their way systematically and efficiently into the commercial sector. We were told that any attempt, at present, to take the results of government-conducted research with a view to commercializing them is a fool's errand. We heard repeatedly during our interviews that it is frustrating and difficult to find out what is going on in government R&D. Publication of encyclopaedic listings of research projects is not an especially useful way to disseminate substantive information, and several attempts to set up information desks have met with failure.

The Task Force believes it is necessary to investigate the opportunity for improvement in this regard. An approach that appeals to us would be to identify a sample of a half-dozen or so high-potential opportunities that emerge in government laboratories and, perhaps with the Forum participation, use them as tests to determine whether good, quick, and cost-efficient approaches to commercialization are available.

---

*A.B. Supapol and D.G. McFetridge, *An Analysis of the Federal Make-or-Buy Policy*, Discussion Paper No. 217, Economic Council of Canada, June 1982.

Funding for Others' R&D Activities

The second important way government can enhance the effectiveness of Canada's R&D spending is by redirecting its tax incentives, its own funding of universities, and various block grants and support programs. Again on the basis of interview evidence, the Task Force recommends that:

1. Alternatives to tax-incentive support for research and development be considered. Small companies (those in greatest need of R&D support) are either not yet profitable, or have other forms of tax deferral, such as capital equipment projects, available to them. Thus, tax-reduction incentives are useless to them now. Specifically, we suggest reconsidering the proposal to allow small companies to transfer R&D tax shelters to other companies or institutions, recognizing that such a change in policy would have to incorporate new ways to reduce the kind of abuses that have occurred in the past.

2. Consistent with the findings of the Wright Report,* the Task Force believes universities should also be given some incentive to cooperative actively with corporations. This can probably be done most effectively by providing added incentives to universities when they obtain corporate funding.

3. The government should rethink its approach to broad-scale support of universities, establishing programs that will:
   - encourage corporations and universities to increase their professional competence in specific relevant areas of research
   - lead to the creation of Centres of Initiative
   - address Canada's R&D talent shortfall.

4. NSERC should be permitted to restructure its formula system for grants so as to provide universities with funds to recover overhead costs which are generated by the projects undertaken, in addition to the actual research funds.

> "Small companies can't use tax incentives as effectively as large ones; consequently government needs to look at much more direct granting rather than indirect tax incentive systems."
> CORPORATE CEO

> "Government should provide the overhead costs, not just the basic costs."
> CORPORATE CEO

*Task Force on Federal Policies and Programs for Technology Development—report to the Honourable Edward C. Lumley, Minister of State Science and Technology, July 1984.,

4

THE FORUM'S COMMITMENT

Because mere study and debate by themselves are unlikely to produce real change, and because real conviction as to the benefits of corporate-university relationships will come only through experience, the Task Force believes that the Corporate-Higher Education Forum should lead by example. The Forum should, therefore, begin a long-term program that will, we are convinced, result in richer, more rewarding relationships between universities and corporations and, equally important, among individual researchers.

Forum Initiatives

The Forum is committed to supporting corporate-university cooperation in the following ways:

1. With government participation, evaluate the opportunity to develop one or more Canadian Centres of Initiative. Specifically, the Forum will:
   - identify those factors that are required for a successful Centre of Initiative in Canada;
   - determine ways to enhance prospects of success for one or more Canadian Centres of Initiative; and
   - work with the participants at the Centre(s) to encourage self-sustaining growth.

2. Solicit government participation in a project designed to translate government R&D activities into commercial products or processes. Specifically, the Forum proposes to work with appropriate government agencies to:
   * identify five or six non-classified government research projects that seem likely candidates for commercialization;
   * work with government and corporate researchers to identify a range of commercial opportunities;
   * screen or review the most promising research projects;
   * act as matchmaker, and help to facilitate agreements for the commercial exploitation of the research projects;
   * based on the experience of the foregoing, develop recommendations as to how government might:
     - routinely monitor and screen its R&D activities for commercial opportunities, and
     - improve mechanisms for interaction with the universities and private sector.

3. Designate a Forum representative to be a corporate-university research resource officer with a responsibility for:
   * monitoring current university/corporate research activity—ie. expand on and update the surveys carried out for *Partnership for Growth* and *Spending Smarter*;
   * identifying outstanding examples of successful corporate-university cooperation, and the reasons for their success;
   * disseminating information relative to the above, perhaps in the form of a regular newsletter; and
   * facilitating interchange between universities and corporations through meetings of corporate and university researchers and by monitoring the effectiveness of Forum members' initiatives and reporting to members.

4. Investigate and implement a "Window into Universities" program, perhaps using NSERC and Medical Research Council data as a starting point.

5. Designate an ad-hoc Task Force to develop a brief, standard short-term R&D research contract document (ideally, not more than two pages in length) which specifies acceptable ("mean" or "average") expectations in all areas of joint activity, thus enabling corporations and universities to adapt the standard form to their specific projects. Ideally, such a Task Force will include representation from research, legal, and administrative staffs of Forum members.

6. Each year award a cash prize* of up to $25,000 to two researchers, one each from a university and a corporation, who represent outstanding examples of productive corporate-university cooperation. The awarding of this honour would be supported by an appropriate media program designed to gain wide visibility.

Forum Member Initiatives

To make their initiatives both credible and inspirational, Forum members have ensured that their projects will:

1. consist of new programs or significant extensions of programs already in place, not merely existing programs with new labels;

2. note explicitly how success—or failure—is to be measured; and

3. specify a clear target date.

The following commitments to action were made by Forum members following the 1985 annual meeting at which *Spending Smarter* was presented by the Task Force, and prior to publication.

---

*To be funded perhaps by the Forum or by a consortium of Canada's large R&D spenders.

Figure 7 Forum Member Initiatives

Member	Initiatives	Criteria for Success	Deadline/Time Frame	Rationale
Bell Canada	• Designate a university professor to R&D Review Committee	Decision to review appointment or to add others	2 years	Reduction in barriers to working with universities; obtain hard information about universities' capabilities
	• Double spending by matching specific university research contracts with equal unrestricted basic-research dollars, in return for periodic reports of findings	Useful ideas generated	3 years	Technical insights into high-priority areas PR in the academic community
Dalhousie University	• Establishment of NSERC/Industry (Petro Canada Resources) Chair in Marine Geology	NSERC/Industry Chairs programme review criteria	Interim review after 2 years—then 5 year review	Self Explanatory
	• Establishment, with other institutions, of an Institute of Biotechnology managed by a Board having industry representative	Review by institutions concerned of progress in establishment of Institute and of links with industry	Review after 5 years	Self Explanatory
	• Establishment of joint office with Mount Saint Vincent University to service Co-op Education programmes for placement of students with business/industry for "work terms"	Review of effective placement of the students—by institutions concerned and Canada Manpower	One year	Self Explanatory

Dalhousie University (cont'd.)	• Special study to be initiated to consider more integrated ties with representatives of industry/corporate sector to facilitate transfer of special services and research outputs of interest to industry/corporations	Consideration of report from study by regular university process and with outside advice	Spring 1986	Possibilities of greater technology transfer previously considered but now timely to review again in light of developing interests within university and industry/business developments within the region
Imperial Oil	• Review of $900,000 university grant program	Greater relevance to the program	This year	Refocus the program toward more relevant activities
	• Initiate relationships with universities on emerging technologies	Maintenance of technological window	This year	Keep current in new technology
	• Co-establish Sarnia Centre for Science and Technology	Organization in place Initial program	2 years	Establish centre of excellence in chemical and petroleum process industry
McGill University	• Act as a catalyst in the formation of a group for the promotion and development of a Centre of Initiative in the Greater Montreal Area	Commitment from various levels of government, local private sector organizations and local universities to participate in the group and to undertake basic planning for promotion and development	This year	The Greater Montreal Area already possesses three of the five "key success factors" identified in Figure 2 – outstanding science/engineering universities with strong corporate support – major corporate and governmental research and development facilities – an attractive city with most of the necessary attributes

Figure 7 (Continued)

Member	Initiatives	Criteria for Success	Deadline/Time Frame	Rationale
University of Regina	• Set up a chair in telecommunications in partnership with SASK TEL and NSERC	Development of joint research and development projects of benefit to the industrial partner and the university	Five years	Many needs in the telecommunication sector in the province are not now being handled, and this initiative will develop research expertise for the province and the university
SED Systems	• Fund a chair at University of Saskatchewan for research in telecommunications, particularly in the field of microwaves	A consultative centre for the company	5 years	Need to create a "climate" to attract and hold technical people in the community
	• One graduate scholarship; five undergraduate scholarships	Enhance local supply for recruitment		
	• Contract research	General upgrading of professional staff		
SNC	• Joint research project with UBC on coal gasification	Allowing SNC to build jointly with Coal Research Institute of Peking a demonstration plant.	2 years	Penetration of coal gasification market in China.
	• Joint research project with École Polytechnic on a biochemical reactor	Adequate data generated for large scale system	2 years	Technical insights into emerging field
	• Joint research project with McGill on reverse osmosis	Generation of fundamental data	4 years	Basic understanding of scientific phenomena
	• Joint research project with McGill on solvation of coal	Understanding of principles of coal chemistry	6 years	Basic research on coal chemistry

SNC (cont'd.)	• Joint research project for the enrichment of coal by oil agglomeration	Data generated for development of process	2 years	Technical insights into important field
	• Designate one or more university professors to R&D review committee	Constructive criticism of SNC's R&D program	2 years	External view of emerging technical areas
	• Actively encourage qualified staff of SNC to hold appointments of auxiliary professor at universities	Appointments in place at universities	Long-term	Good relations with universities, bringing industrial view points to staff and students
University of Toronto	• Designate a Research Relations Coordinator reporting directly to the Vice-President, Research	Improved understanding by industry of university research base; greater number of specific research contracts or agreements	Has just been implemented; success to be reviewed in three years	Industry needs known, central contact point; more information on University research should be available to industry
	• Develop new computerized data base accessible according to the research interest of the private sector and government	Existence of up-to-date database.	Two years, beginning in the fall of 1985	Existing data base is oriented entirely towards internal administrative needs and not very useful for identifying quickly areas of specific interest to the private sector
	• Extend financial support to the University of Toronto Innovations Foundation for a second five-year period	Additional growth in the commercialization of inventions; financial self-sufficiency for the Foundation	1985 to 1990	Commercialization is a lengthy process, the financial returns from which may not appear for many years; enormous flow of inventions and inventive activity at U of T
	• Through Innovations Foundation, develop data base of industry research interests and contact people	Ability quickly to relate a University research project to specific companies and specific people in those companies	Two years	Current inability systematically to inform researchers and industry of mutual interests

Figure 7 (Continued)

Member	Initiatives	Criteria for Success	Deadline/Time Frame	Rationale
University of Toronto (cont'd.)	• Host or co-sponsor a series of industry-university interface conferences	Research contracts or licensing agreements	1986 onwards	Need for better and more specific information flow
University of Western Ontario	• Establish Commercial Development Officer on campus (sponsored by IDEA)	Increased interaction with industry	3 years	Foster commercial development of University research
	• Develop keyword inventory of research expertise	Increased interaction; better information for industry	1 year	Easier access to university expertise
Xerox	• Donation of equipment to a university to further development work in the area of artificial intelligence	Specific applications produced	2 years	To increase knowledge of specific applications of artificial intelligence

SURVEY RESULTS AND ANALYSES

A Corporate R&D Expenditure Patterns

The Forum's survey of corporate R&D expenditures in Canada covered primarily large corporations (Figure A-1) representing approximately 83 percent of the projected expenditures of leading performers of R&D as identified by *The Financial Post* (Figure A-2). Survey results have been used to estimate, for the first time, the size and composition of Canadian corporate spending in the universities and to draw some comparisions between Canadian- and foreign-controlled companies.

NOTES ON METHODOLOGY

The estimates of R&D spending in this section are based on straight-line extrapolations of spending patterns identified by the Forum's Canadian Corporate R&D Expenditure Survey. Forty-nine leading performers of R&D in Canada, foreign- and Canadian-controlled, detailed how and where their spending took place—by country of expenditure, type of laboratory used, stage of research undertaken, and the disciplines involved. The data covered each company's most recent fiscal year which, for the most part, was calendar year 1984.

The estimate of $3,062.4 million, representing the overall total R&D spending in North America, results from grossing up the Statistics Canada estimate of 1984 domestic R&D expenditure of $2,673 million according to the Survey's relationship of the two types of R&D spending in Canada to that in the United States. Similarly, the estimate of spending in North American universities is based on their share of R&D spending, as reported by the companies, applied to the estimated overall expenditures in Canada and the United States.

Throughout, total spending includes both directed and non-directed R&D support. *Directed* support is defined as project-related contractual research; *non-directed* support, as funded chairs, grants, scholarships, equipment, etc.

SUMMARY OF CONCLUSIONS

The following conclusions summarize the results illustrated in the Figures. Throughout this section percentages may not add to 100 because figures have been rounded.

1. **Corporations Support Universities to the Tune of $52 Million**
   - The Forum survey covers 56 percent of the 1984 Statistics Canada estimate of directed corporate R&D expenditures in Canada, and reflects the national sectoral distribution of spending (Figure A-3).
   - Our best estimate of the total *directed* R&D spending by Canadian corporations with North American universities is $22.0 million, of which approximately $19.1 million is spent in Canada (Figure A-4).
   - All gifts, donations, and other *non-directed* funding and support total an estimated additional $30.4 million, of which $30.0 million goes to Canadian universities primarily from foreign-controlled companies (Figure A-5).
   - The estimated total Canadian corporate R&D support is $52.4 million, of which $49.1 million goes to Canadian universities primarily from foreign-controlled companies (Figure A-6).

2. **Corporate Directed R&D Expenditures are Highly Concentrated**
   - Canadian corporate directed R&D expenditures are highly concentrated by country and disci-

pline and are almost exclusively spent in-house (Figure A-7).
- Engineering expenditures, which represent nearly two-thirds of Canadian corporate directed R&D expenditures, are mainly in the Development stage (Figure A-8).
- Very little of Canadian corporate directed R&D is spent outside the companies' own laboratories; universities receive only one-third of the dollars that go to commercial labs, but receive more than non-profit and government labs (Figure A-9).

3. But Their Spending with Universities Does Not Fit the Overall Pattern
- More than 80 percent of Canadian corporate directed R&D expenditures are in the Engineering and Computer fields in the Applied and Development stages (Figure A-10).
- Canadian corporate directed R&D with universities is different—concentrated in Basic and Applied, mainly in Engineering and Science for Canadian-controlled companies, and Computer disciplines for foreign-controlled companies (Figure A-11).

4. Foreign Companies Provide more Support than Canadian Companies
- Support by Canadian- and foreign-controlled companies for university directed R&D is consistent with their shares of overall directed R&D, but subsidiaries of foreign companies provide more than two-thirds of the *total* R&D support to Canadian universities (Figure A-12).
- Average *directed* R&D spending with Canadian universities is approximately eight-tenths of one percent of total directed R&D spending, principally from companies with higher than average R&D spending levels (Figure A-13).
- Adding *non-directed* expenditure to *directed* R&D expenditure increases support by more than two and one-half times (Figure A-14).
- The level of *total support* for university R&D activity from foreign-controlled companies is several times more than that from Canadian-controlled companies (Figure A-15).

Proportion of the Financial Post 500 Companies

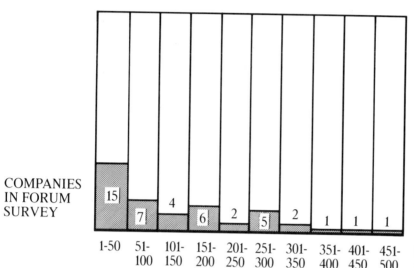

COMPANIES
IN FORUM
SURVEY

THE FINANCIAL POST RANKINGS

Plus five others
- Bytec-Comterm
- Geac
- Lumonics
- Syncrude
- Sydney
  Development

Source: The Financial Post 500, 1984

Observation: **The Forum survey respondents are primarily large corporations.**

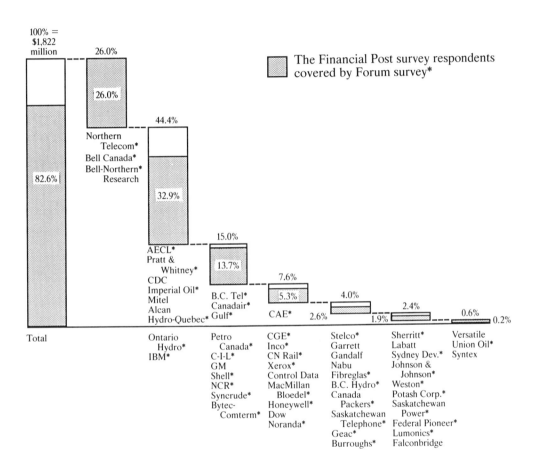

Figure A–2   **Comparison of Forum and the Financial Post Surveys of 1984 R&D Spending in Canada**
Percent

The Financial Post survey respondents covered by Forum survey*

100% = $1,822 million

	26.0%	44.4%	15.0%	7.6%	4.0%	2.4%	0.6%
82.6%	26.0%	32.9%	13.7%	5.3%	1.9%		0.2%
				2.6%			

| Total | Ontario Hydro* IBM* | Petro Canada* C-I-L* GM Shell* NCR* Syncrude* Bytec- Comterm* | CGE* Inco* CN Rail* Xerox* Control Data MacMillan Bloedel* Honeywell* Dow Noranda* | Stelco* Garrett Gandalf Nabu Fibreglas* B.C. Hydro* Canada Packers* Saskatchewan Telephone* Geac* Burroughs* | Sherritt* Labatt Sydney Dev.* Johnson & Johnson* Weston* Potash Corp.* Saskatchewan Power* Federal Pioneer* Lumonics* Falconbridge | Versatile Union Oil* Syntex |

(bars labelled, left to right): Northern Telecom*, Bell Canada*, Bell-Northern* Research; AECL*, Pratt & Whitney*, CDC, Imperial Oil*, Mitel, Alcan, Hydro-Quebec*; B.C. Tel*, Canadair*, Gulf*; CAE*

*Respondents to Forum survey

Source: The Financial Post R&D Survey, May 5, 1984; Forum Corporate R&D Expenditure Survey

Observation: **The Forum Corporate R&D Expenditure Survey covers nearly 83 percent of the projected expenditures of leading performers of R&D in Canada as identified by *The Financial Post.***

Figure A–3 Forum Survey Expenditures Compared to 1984 Statistics Canada Estimate
Percent

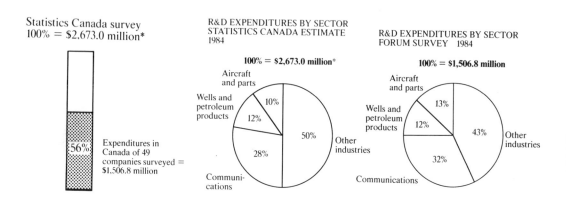

Statistics Canada survey
100% = $2,673.0 million*

Expenditures in Canada of 49 companies surveyed = $1,506.8 million

R&D EXPENDITURES BY SECTOR
STATISTICS CANADA ESTIMATE
1984
100% = $2,673.0 million*

Aircraft and parts 10%
Wells and petroleum products 12%
Communications 28%
Other industries 50%

R&D EXPENDITURES BY SECTOR
FORUM SURVEY 1984
100% = $1,506.8 million

Aircraft and parts 13%
Wells and petroleum products 12%
Communications 32%
Other industries 43%

*Excludes some *non-directed* support of universities—e.g., gifts of equipment.

Source: McKinsey analysis

Observation: **Forum survey covers 56 percent of Statistics Canada 1984 estimate of *directed* corporate R&D expenditures in Canada and reflects the national sectoral distribution of spending.**

Figure A–4 Distribution of Estimated Canadian Corporate *Directed* R&D Spending in North American Universities 1984 100% = $22 million
Percent

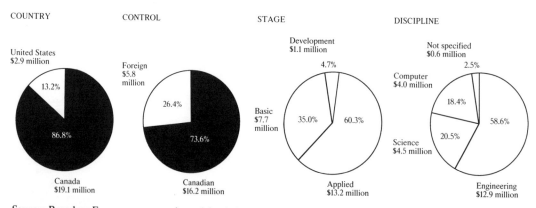

COUNTRY

United States $2.9 million 13.2%
Canada $19.1 million 86.8%

CONTROL

Foreign $5.8 million 26.4%
Canadian $16.2 million 73.6%

STAGE

Development $1.1 million 4.7%
Basic $7.7 million 35.0%
Applied $13.2 million 60.3%

DISCIPLINE

Not specified $0.6 million 2.5%
Computer $4.0 million 18.4%
Science $4.5 million 20.5%
Engineering $12.9 million 58.6%

Source: Based on Forum survey results and Statistics Canada estimates; McKinsey analysis.

Observation: **Our best estimate of the total *directed* R&D spending by Canadian corporations with North American universities is about $22.0 million, of which about $19.1 million is spent in Canada primarily by Canadian-controlled companies.**

Figure A–5   **Distribution of Estimated Canadian Corporate *Non-Directed* R&D Support to North American Universities 1984   100% = $30.4 million**
Percent

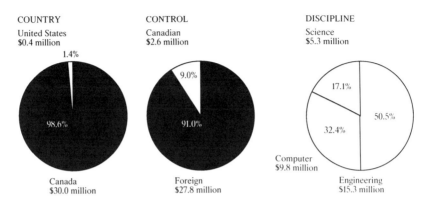

COUNTRY

United States
$0.4 million

1.4%

98.6%

Canada
$30.0 million

CONTROL

Canadian
$2.6 million

9.0%

91.0%

Foreign
$27.8 million

DISCIPLINE

Science
$5.3 million

17.1%

50.5%

32.4%

Computer
$9.8 million

Engineering
$15.3 million

Note: Distribution by stage is not possible because of general use of *non-directed* R&D support.

Source: Based on Forum survey results and Statistics Canada estimates; McKinsey analysis.

Observation: **All gifts, donations, and other *non-directed* funding and support total an estimated additional $30.4 million, of which $30.0 million goes to Canadian universities primarily from foreign-controlled companies.**

Figure A–6   **Distribution of Estimated *Total* Canadian Corporate R&D Support to North American Universities 1984   100% = $52.4 million**
Percent

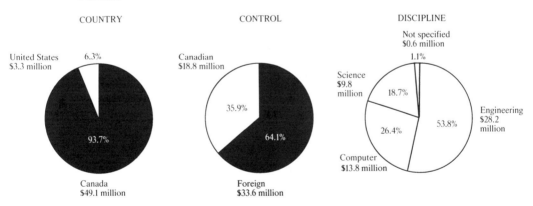

COUNTRY

United States
$3.3 million

6.3%

93.7%

Canada
$49.1 million

CONTROL

Canadian
$18.8 million

35.9%

64.1%

Foreign
$33.6 million

DISCIPLINE

Not specified
$0.6 million

1.1%

Science
$9.8
million

18.7%

26.4%

53.8%

Engineering
$28.2
million

Computer
$13.8 million

Note: Distribution by stage is not possible because of general use of *non-directed* R&D support.

Source: Based on Forum survey results and Statistics Canada estimates; McKinsey analysis.

Observation: **The estimated *total* Canadian corporate R&D support is $52.4 million of which $49.1 million goes to Canadian universities, primarily from foreign-controlled companies.**

Figure A–7 Distribution of Canadian Corporate *Directed* R&D Spending in North America*
1984 100% = $1,709 million
Percent

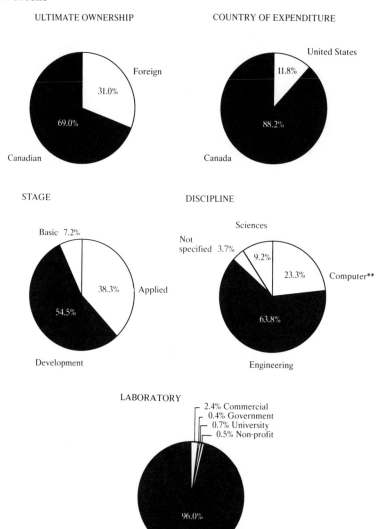

ULTIMATE OWNERSHIP

Foreign
31.0%
69.0%
Canadian

COUNTRY OF EXPENDITURE

United States
11.8%
88.2%
Canada

STAGE

Basic 7.2%
38.3% Applied
54.5%
Development

DISCIPLINE

Sciences
Not specified 3.7%
9.2%
23.3% Computer**
63.8%
Engineering

LABORATORY

2.4% Commercial
0.4% Government
0.7% University
0.5% Non-profit
96.0%
In-house

*98.3% of total *directed* R&D spending is made in North America.
**When expenditures by Bell Canada group of companies are excluded, computer share is approximately 9.0%.

Source: McKinsey analysis

Observation: **Canadian corporate *directed* R&D expenditures are highly concentrated by country and discipline and are almost exclusively spent in-house.**

Figure A – 8 **Distribution of Canadian Corporate *Directed* R&D Spending by Discipline by Stage – North America   1984 Forum Survey**
Percent

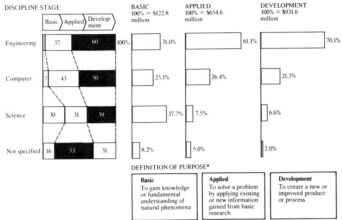

*As defined in the survey

Source: McKinsey analysis

Observation: **Engineering expenditures, which represent nearly two-thirds of Canadian corporate *directed* R&D expenditures, are mainly in the development stage.**

Figure A – 9 **Distribution of Canadian Corporate *Directed* R&D Spending by Discipline by Location – North America   1984 Forum Survey $ Millions**

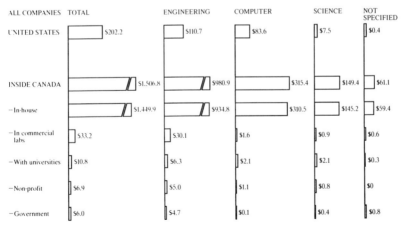

Source: McKinsey analysis

Observation: **Very little of Canadian corporate *directed* R&D is spent outside the companies' own laboratories; universities receive only one-third of the dollars that go to commercial laboratories, but receive more than non-profit and government laboratories.**

Canadian- and Foreign-Controlled Companies' *Directed* **R&D Expenditures by Discipline and Stage in Canada 1984 Forum Survey**
$ Millions

☐ Canadian controlled $986.3 million
▨ Foreign controlled $520.5 million

STAGE	ENGINEERING	COMPUTER	SCIENCE	NOT SPECIFIED	TOTAL
BASIC	$30.1 $3.1 Canadian Foreign controlled controlled	$25.7 $0.1 Canadian Foreign controlled controlled	$39.1 $6.4 Canadian Foreign controlled controlled	$9.8 $0.2 Canadian Foreign controlled controlled	$104.7 $9.8 Canadian Foreign controlled controlled
APPLIED	$292.6 $71.6	$116.5 $9.1	$28.9 $15.7	$30.4 $2.0	$468.4 $98.4
DEVELOP-MENT	$280.3 $303.2	$85.2 $78.8	$34.8 $24.5	$12.9 $5.8	$413.2 $412.3
TOTAL	$603.0 $377.9	$227.4 $88.0	$102.8 $46.6	$53.1 $8.0	$986.3 $520.5

Source: McKinsey analysis

Observation: **More than 80 percent of Canadian corporate** *directed* **R&D expenditures in Canada are in the Engineering and Computer fields in the Applied and Development stages.**

70

Figure A–11   **Canadian- and Foreign-Controlled Companies'** *Directed* **R&D Expenditures with Canadian Universities by Discipline and Stage 1984   Forum Survey $ Millions**

☐ Canadian controlled $7.8 million

▨ Foreign controlled $3.0 million

STAGE	ENGINEERING		COMPUTER		SCIENCE		NOT SPECIFIED		TOTAL	
	Canadian controlled	Foreign controlled	Canadian controlled	Foreign controlled	Canadian controlled	Foreign controlled	Canadian controlled	Foreign controlled	Canadian controlled	Foreign controlled
BASIC	$0.825	$0.750	$0.337		$1.342	$0.177	$0.150	$0.012	$2.654	$0.939
APPLIED	$4.084	$0.242		$1.578	$0.521		$0.150	$0.001	$4.755	$1.821
DEVELOP-MENT	$0.370	$0.057	$0.150		$0.007				$0.377	$0.207
TOTAL	$5.279	$1.049	$0.337	$1.728	$1.870	$0.177	$0.300	$0.013	$7.786	$2.967

Source: McKinsey analysis

Observation: **Canadian corporate** *directed* **R&D with Canadian universities is different – concentrated in Basic and Applied – mainly in Engineering and Science for Canadian-controlled companies, and Computer disciplines for foreign-controlled companies.**

Distribution of Canadian Corporate *Directed* R&D by Control
1984 Forum Survey
Percent

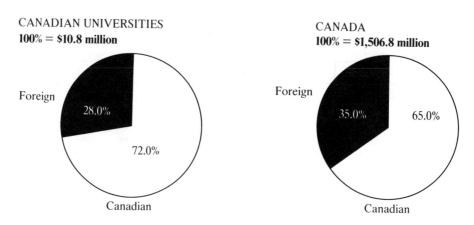

CANADIAN UNIVERSITIES
100% = $10.8 million

CANADA
100% = $1,506.8 million

Foreign
28.0%
72.0%
Canadian

Foreign
35.0%   65.0%
Canadian

Distribution of *Total* Canadian Corporate R&D Support by Control
1984 Forum Survey
Percent

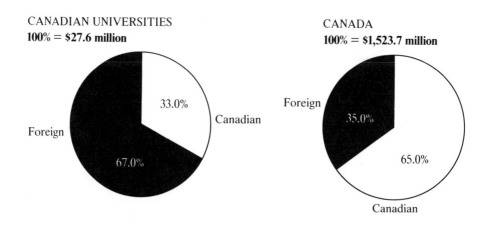

CANADIAN UNIVERSITIES
100% = $27.6 million

CANADA
100% = $1,523.7 million

33.0%
Canadian
Foreign
67.0%

Foreign
35.0%
65.0%
Canadian

Note: The Forum Survey had 49 corporate respondents of which 32 were Canadian and 17 were foreign controlled. *Directed* R&D at universities was supported by 22 Canadian- and 10 foreign-controlled companies. Overall support for university R&D was made by 25 Canadian- and 11 foreign-controlled companies.

Source: McKinsey analysis

Observation: **Support by Canadian- and foreign-controlled companies for university *directed* R&D is consistent with their shares of overall *directed* R&D, but subsidiaries of foreign companies provide significantly more than two-thirds of *total* R&D support to Canadian universities.**

Figure A–13 *Directed* R&D Spending by Canadian Corporations 1984

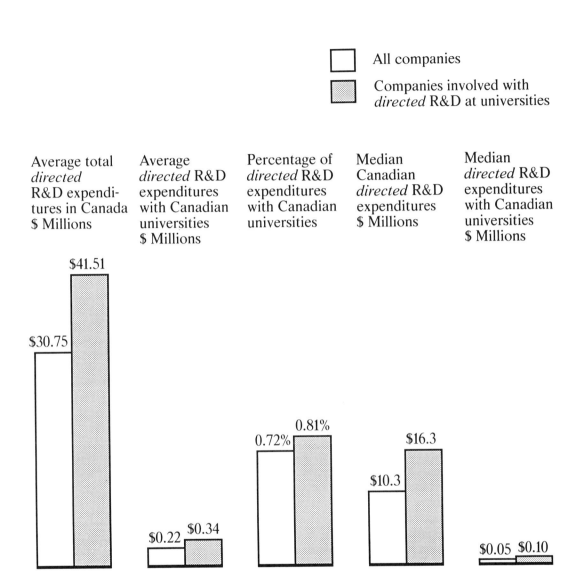

☐ All companies

▨ Companies involved with *directed* R&D at universities

Average total *directed* R&D expenditures in Canada $ Millions

Average *directed* R&D expenditures with Canadian universities $ Millions

Percentage of *directed* R&D expenditures with Canadian universities

Median Canadian *directed* R&D expenditures $ Millions

Median *directed* R&D expenditures with Canadian universities $ Millions

$41.51
$30.75
$0.22 $0.34
0.72% 0.81%
$10.3 $16.3
$0.05 $0.10

Source: McKinsey analysis

Observation: **Average *directed* R&D spending with Canadian universities is approximately 0.8 percent of total directed R&D spending, principally from companies with higher than average R&D spending levels.**

Figure A–14 **Canadian Corporate Support of Canadian University R&D and Related Disciplines   1984 Forum Survey $ Millions**

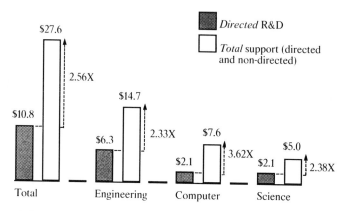

Source: McKinsey analysis

Observation: **Including *non-directed* expenditure increases support by more than two and one-half times.**

Figure A–15 ***Total* University R&D Support from Participating Corporations by Control 1984 Forum Survey**

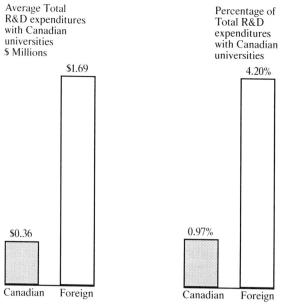

Source: McKinsey analysis

Observation: **The level of *total support* for university R&D activity from foreign-controlled companies is several times more than that from Canadian-controlled companies.**

Corporate R&D Survey Respondents

Alberta Energy Company Ltd.
Atomic Energy of Canada Limited
Bell Canada*
Bell-Northern Research Ltd.*
Bombardier Inc.
British Columbia Hydro
   and Power Authority
British Columbia Telephone Co.
Burroughs Canada
Bytec-Comterm Inc.
CAE Industries Ltd.
C-I-L Inc.
Canada Packers Inc.
Canadair Limited
Canadian General Electric Co. Ltd.
Canadian Marconi Company
Canadian National Railway
Connaught Laboratories Limited
Dofasco Inc.
Federal Pioneer Limited
Fiberglas Canada Inc.
Geac Computer Corporation Limited
George Weston Limited
Gulf Canada Ltd.
Honeywell Limited/Limitée
Hydro-Quebec

IBM Canada Ltd.
Imperial Oil Limited
Inco Limited
Johnson & Johnson Inc.
Lumonics Inc.
MacMillan Bloedel Limited
NCR Canada Ltd./Ltée.
Noranda Mines Limited
Northern Telecom Limited*
NOVA/An Alberta Corporation
Ontario Hydro
Petro-Canada Inc.
Polysar Limited
Potash Corporation of Saskatchewan
Pratt & Whitney Canada Inc.
The SNC Group
Saskatchewan Power Corporation
Saskatchewan Telecommunications
Shell Canada Limited
Sherritt Gordon Mines Ltd.
Spar Aerospace Ltd.
Stelco Inc.
Sydney Development Corporation
Syncrude Canada Ltd.
Union Oil Company of Canada
Xerox Canada Inc.

---

*Survey response treated as single company

B External Funding Patterns for University R&D

In parallel to the survey of corporations, the Forum conducted a survey of 14 universities that represent approximately 55 percent of the total external research funding for Canadian Universities (Figure B-1). The universities sampled are distributed fairly evenly across the 20 largest sponsored research universities (Figure B-2).

NOTES ON METHODOLOGY

The estimate of R&D spending in this section is based on straight-line extrapolations of spending patterns identified by the Forum's Survey of External Funding for University Research and Development. Fourteen universities provided information on how and from whom they received R&D support. Their breakdowns covered government, corporate, non-profit, commercial revenue and other sources and identified whether the support was in kind—i.e., equipment or financial (e.g., contracts, grants, or fellowships). These data covered their most recent fiscal year, which for the most part was 1983-84.

The estimate of total *corporate* support for Canadian university R&D is $51.7 million. This is based on the *Survey* relationship of corporate to overall external funding as applied to the *total* $664.7 million of sponsored research received by Canadian universities and colleges in 1982-83, the most recent year for which data are available from Statistics Canada.

This survey marks the first attempt by universities to provide a comprehensive accounting of external funding for R&D at their institutions and affiliated research institutes/centres. The institutions regard their individual data as accurate. However, comparisons between universities are subject to differences in academic programs (e.g., the presence/absence of medical faculties), coverage of affiliated research organizations, accounting practices, and their definitions of disciplines, sources, etc.

SUMMARY OF CONCLUSIONS

The principal results of the survey follow. Throughout this section percentages may not add to 100 because figures have been rounded.

1. External Funding Sources are Highly Concentrated

- Federal and Provincial Government sources represent almost 80.0 percent of university external funding, while all corporate sources represent the fourth largest component at 7.8 percent (Figure B-3).
- Within each of the four major sources of external funds there is a dominant supplier: NSERC, Provincial Government contracts, Canadian companies, and Canadian non-profit organizations (Figure B-4).

2. Universities Receive $51 Million in Corporate Support

- All forms of corporate support average 7.8 percent of universities' external funding, although the range is from a high of 27.0 percent to a low of 3.0 percent (Figure B-5).
- Our best estimate of the total size of corporate (foreign and Canadian) support, received by Canadian universities, based on university responses, is $51.7 million (Figure B-6).

3. Corporate Funding of Universities is Selective

- Waterloo has been more successful than other universities at attracting corporate sponsorship (Figure B-7).
- Almost 80 percent of all external support is in the form of grants, fellowships, and scholarships spread across all disciplines (Figure B-8).
- Corporate support is concentrated by discipline and is heavily skewed toward contractual relationships (Figure B-9).

Figure B–1 Forum Survey of External R&D Funding Compared to Statistics Canada Percent

Statistics Canada survey
100% = $664.7 million

55%

External funding
of research and
development at
14 universities =
$365.3 million*

*Forum survey includes $5 million in equipment, which is excluded in Statistics Canada data

Note: Statistics Canada reports income for sponsored research in *all* disciplines; the Forum survey focused solely on funding for R&D in the natural, physical and health sciences, engineering, agriculture and forestry disciplines

Source: Financial Statistics of Universities and Colleges, 1982-83—Canadian Association of University Business Officers and Statistics Canada; Forum Survey of External Funding for University Research and Development; McKinsey analysis

Observation : **1984 Forum survey covers 55 percent of funding received for *all* R&D at Canadian universities in 1982-83, the most recent year for which data are available.**

Figure B–2 Comparison of Forum Survey to Funds for Sponsored Research at Top 20 Universities Percent

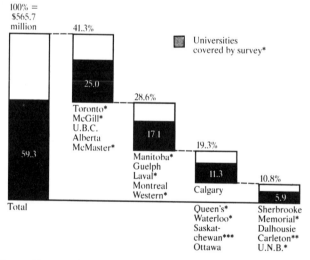

*Respondents to Forum Survey of External Funding for University Research and Development in natural, physical and health sciences, agricultural and forestry
**Carleton data are the average of data for 1982-84
***Saskatchewan data are for 1982-83

Source: Financial Statistics of Universities and Colleges, 1982-83—Canadian Association of University Business Officers and Statistics Canada

Observation: **The Forum survey covers 60 percent of the funds received by the top 20 university recipients of sponsored research funding.**

Figure B–3   External Funding of Canadian Universities by Source: 1983-84
Percent

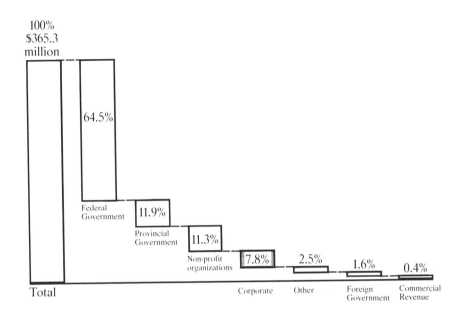

FUNDING SOURCE DESCRIPTION
- *Federal Government* grants, contracts, fellowships from Natural Sciences and Engineering Research Council, National Research Council, Medical Research Council, and other departments
- *Provincial Government* grants, contracts, fellowships from departments and provincial research organizations
- *Corporate* support such as contracts, grants, scholarships, chairs, endowments, equipment, and campaign funds from Canadian and foreign companies and industrial associations
- *Non-profit* grants, fellowships, and contracts from Canadian and foreign associations and foundations
- *Other* donations from individuals, income from endowment investments and other miscellaneous sources
- *Foreign government* contracts and grants
- *Commercial Revenue* royalties and income from the sale of products and processes

Source: McKinsey analysis

Observation: **Federal and Provincial Government sources represent almost 80.0 percent of university external funding, while all corporate sources represent the fourth largest component at 7.8 percent.**

Figure B–4 Sources of External Funding

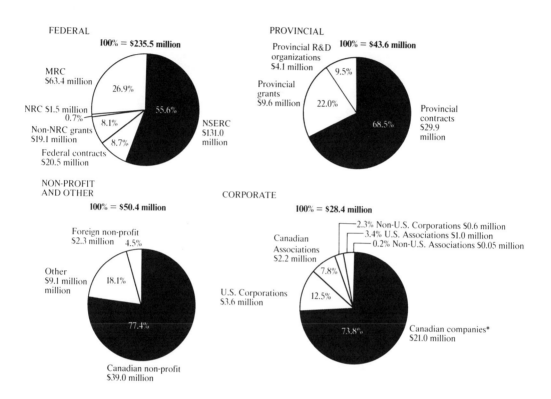

*Respondents were unable to distinguish effectively between Canadian- and foreign-controlled companies in Canada

Source: Forum Survey of External Funding for University R&D; McKinsey analysis

Observation: **Within each of the four major sources of external funds, there is a dominant supplier – NSERC, Provincial Government contracts, Canadian companies, and Canadian non-profit organizations.**

Figure B–5   External Sources of Funding for R&D by Institution   1983-84 $ Millions
Percent

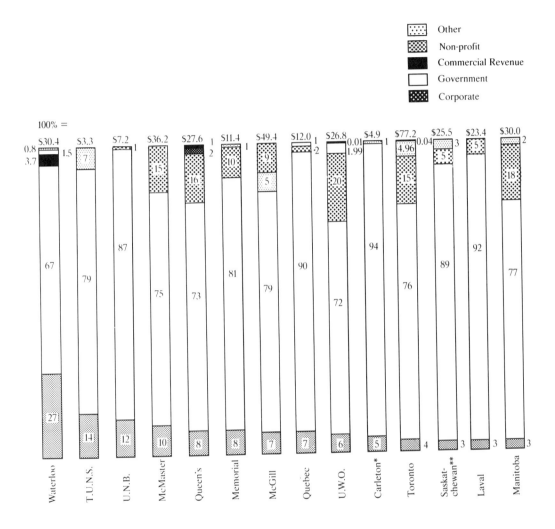

*Carleton data are the average of data for 1982-84
**Saskatchewan data are for 1982-83

Source: Forum Survey of External Funding for University R&D; McKinsey analysis

Observation: **All forms of corporate support average 7.8 percent of universities' external funding, although the range is from a high of 27.0 percent to a low of 3.0 percent.**

Figure B–6 **Estimated Total Corporate Support for Canadian University R&D**
Percent

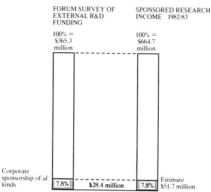

FORUM SURVEY OF
EXTERNAL R&D
FUNDING

SPONSORED RESEARCH
INCOME 1982-83

100% =
$365.3
million

100% =
$664.7
million

Corporate
sponsorship of all
kinds

7.8% $28.4 million

Estimate
7.8% $51.7 million

Source: Financial Statistics of Universities and Colleges, 1982-85—Canadian Association of University Business Officers and Statistics Canada; McKinsey analysis

Observation: **Our best estimate of the total size of corporate support received by Canadian universities, based on university responses, is $51.7 million.**

Figure B–7 **Corporate Funding per Faculty Member by Institution $ Thousands**

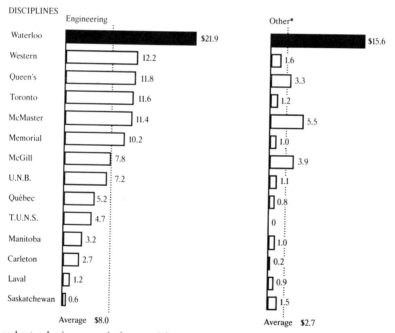

DISCIPLINES

	Engineering	Other*
Waterloo	$21.9	$15.6
Western	12.2	1.6
Queen's	11.8	3.3
Toronto	11.6	1.2
McMaster	11.4	5.5
Memorial	10.2	1.0
McGill	7.8	3.9
U.N.B.	7.2	1.1
Québec	5.2	0.8
T.U.N.S.	4.7	0
Manitoba	3.2	1.0
Carleton	2.7	0.2
Laval	1.2	0.9
Saskatchewan	0.6	1.5
	Average $8.0	Average $2.7

*Other: health and natural sciences, agriculture, and forestry
Source: Statistics Canada Educational Statistics—unpublished data; university reports; Forum survey of external funding for university R&D; McKinsey analysis.

Observation: **Waterloo has done much better than other universities at attracting corporate sponsorship.**

Figure B-8   **All Forms of External Support by Discipline $ Millions**
              Forum Survey

100% = $365.3 million

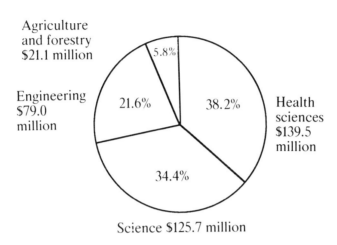

SUPPORT FORM	HEALTH SCIENCES	SCIENCE	ENGI-NEERING	AGRICULTURE AND FORESTRY	TOTAL
Grants, fellowships, and scholarships	$116.2	$100.9	$55.0	$13.1	$285.2
Contracts	23.3	20.7	21.7	8.0	73.7
Equipment	—	2.9	2.1	—	5.0
Commercial revenue	0.01	1.2	0.2	—	1.4
Total	$139.5	$125.7	$79.0	$21.1	$365.3

Source: McKinsey analysis

Observation: **Almost 80 percent of all external support is in the form of grants, fellowships, and scholarships spread across all disciplines.**

External Support by Discipline* Forum Survey
Percent

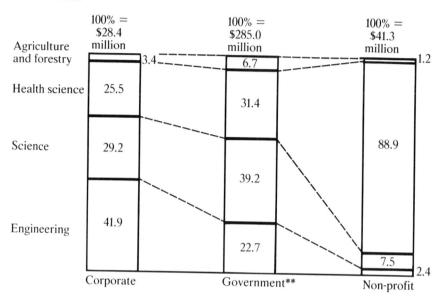

	100% = $28.4 million	100% = $285.0 million	100% = $41.3 million
Agriculture and forestry	3.4	6.7	1.2
Health science	25.5	31.4	
Science	29.2	39.2	88.9
Engineering	41.9	22.7	7.5 / 2.4
	Corporate	Government**	Non-profit

External Support by Type of Relationship* Forum Survey
Percent

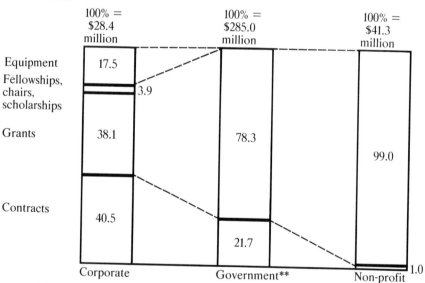

	100% = $28.4 million	100% = $285.0 million	100% = $41.3 million
Equipment	17.5		
Fellowships, chairs, scholarships	3.9		
Grants	38.1	78.3	99.0
Contracts	40.5	21.7	1.0
	Corporate	Government**	Non-profit

*Excludes commercial revenue and other income
**Includes Federal, Provincial, and foreign governments

Source: McKinsey analysis

Observation: ...**corporate support is concentrated in engineering and is heavily skewed toward contractual relationships.**

University R&D Survey Respondents

Carleton University
McGill University
McMaster University
Memorial University
Queen's University
Technical University of Nova Scotia
Université du Québec

Universite Laval
University of Manitoba
University of New Brunswick
University of Saskatchewan
University of Toronto
University of Waterloo
University of Western Ontario

C Membership of Boards by Occupation

Several interviewees cited lack of commitment to inter-action at the top of both corporations and universities as an impediment to better understanding and cooperation. Specifically, not enough business people are on the Boards of universities and not enough academics are on corporate Boards. The facts appear to support at least the contention that little over-lap exists.

- Of the 22 universities surveyed, only 5 have at least half of their Board drawn from the business world and more than half have a third or less (Figure C-1).
- More than half of the business representatives on universities' Boards of Governors are from small companies or are business professionals (Figure C-2).
- Academics represent only 1.3 percent of the Board membership of the major R&D performers in Canada (Figure C-3).

Figure C-1 **Canadian University Boards of Governors by Occupation 1983-84 Percent**

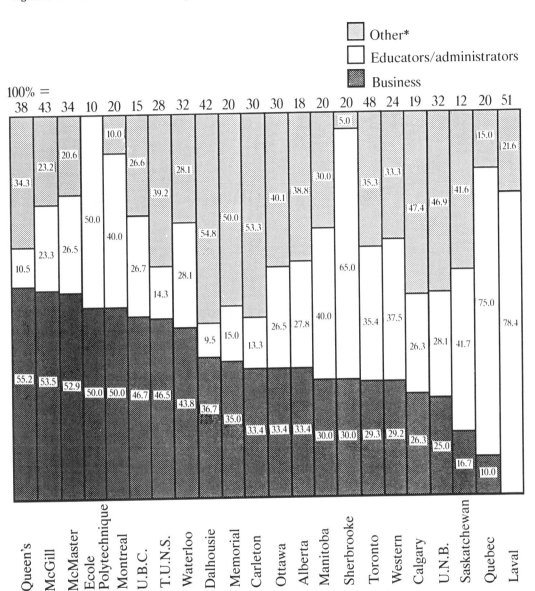

*Other includes lawyers, artists, journalists, homemakers, politicians, students, farmers, union representatives, and civil servants

Source: McKinsey analysis of occupations of voting members of 22 university Boards of Governors

Observation: **Of the 22 universities surveyed, only 5 have at least half of their Board members drawn from the business world and nearly half have a third or less.**

Figure C-2   Corporate Affiliation of Business Members of Canadian University Boards of Governors   1983-84   Percent

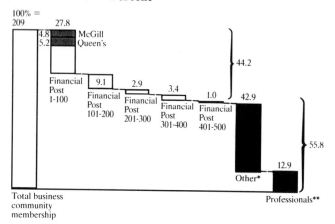

*Other companies: small- and medium-sized companies not ranked by *The Financial Post 500*
**Accountants and consultants

Source: The Financial Post 500—1984; Who's Who In Canada; Who's Who in Business; Directory of Directors; McKinsey analysis of membership of 22 university Boards of Governors

Observation: **More than half of the business representatives on university Boards of Governors are from small companies or are business professionals.**

Figure C-3   Canadian Boards of Directors by Occupation for Leading Corporate Performers of R&D   1983-84   Percent

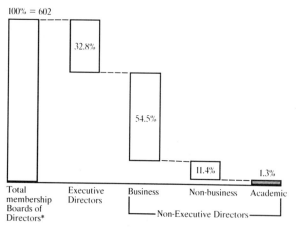

*Boards of Directors of 52 companies identified as leading performers of R&D in Canada

Source: Annual reports; *Directory of Directors; Financial Post R&D Survey,* May 5, 1984

Observation: **Academics represent 1.3 percent of the Board membership of the major R&D performers in Canada.**

APPENDIX A

List of Interviewees

CORPORATE LEADERS

ROD ANDREW
Vice President and
  General Director of Personnel
General Motors of Canada

ALEX G. BALOGH
Group Vice President
Noranda Inc.

LAURENT BEAUDOIN
Chairman and Chief Executive Officer
Bombardier Inc.

ROBERT BLAIR
President and Chief Executive Officer
NOVA/An Alberta Corporation

E.H. BURDETTE
Executive Vice President,
  Planning and Administration
Ontario Hydro

DONALD A. CHISHOLM
Executive Vice President,
  Technology and Innovation
Northern Telecom Limited

C. WILLIAM DANIEL
President and Chief Executive Officer
Shell Canada Ltd.

ROGER DUNN
Vice President
Alberta Energy Company Ltd.

ANDREW EISENHAUER
Chairman and Chief Executive Officer
Atlantic Bridge Company Ltd.

JOHN EVANS
Chairman and Chief Executive Officer
Allelix Inc.

JOHN E. FEICK
President
Novacor Chemicals Ltd. and
    The Alberta Gas Ethylene Company

W.H. HOPPER
Chairman and Chief Executive Officer
Petro-Canada

DOUGLAS J. JAMES
Vice President and General Manager
Lumonics Inc.

FRED KEE
Director, Research and Development
Ontario Hydro

ROBERT KLEIN
*Assistant Vice President,
    Planning and Research*
Canadian Pacific Limited

M.L. LAHN
President and Chief Executive Officer
Canada Trustco Mortgage Company

WALTER F. LIGHT
Chairman and Chief Executive Officer
Northern Telecom Limited

GORDON F. MACFARLANE
Chairman and Chief Executive Officer
British Columbia Telephone Co.

JAMES A. MCDONALD
Vice President, Industry Relations
Canadian Pacific Limited

GEORGE MILLER
General Manager
NOVA/Husky Research Corporation Ltd.

SID MONAGHAN
*Chief, Research
    and Development Support*
Pratt & Whitney Canada Inc.

JOHN H. PANABAKER
Chairman and Chief Executive Officer
The Mutual Life Assurance Company
    of Canada

P.E. PASHLER
Vice President, Technology
Canadian General Electric
    Company Limited

R.R. PICARD
Vice President, Research
Shell Canada Ltd.

PAUL J. PHOENIX
President and Chief Executive Officer
Dofasco Inc.

BERG SCHNEIDER
Research Director
Canada Packers Inc.

SONG SIT
Technical Director
Alberta Energy Company Ltd.

ELVIE L. SMITH
Chairman and Chief Executive Officer
Pratt & Whitney Canada Inc.

VALENTINE N. STOCK
President and Chief Executive Officer
Canada Packers Inc.

IHOR SUCHOVERSKY
*Vice President Research and
    Operations Technology*
Alcan Aluminum Limited

ROMI SZAWLOWKI
*Manager, Manpower Planning
    and Development*
Pratt & Whitney Canada Inc.

PETER TARASSOFF
Director of Research and Development
Noranda Inc.

A.R. TAYLOR
President and Chief Operating Officer
The Royal Bank of Canada

NOEL THOMAS
Director of Research
Dofasco Inc.

E.G. TORRIBLE
*Vice President and Director of
    Technical Personnel Development*
Alcan International Limited

C.M. WILLIAMS
President and Chief Executive Officer
Geac Computer Corporation Limited

JOHN WILSON
Vice President, Fabricating Technology
Alcan International Limited

UNIVERSITY LEADERS

WILLIAM BECKEL
President
Carleton University

CLAIR CALLAGHAN
President
Technical University of Nova Scotia

GEORGE E. CONNELL
President
University of Toronto

ROLAND DORÉ
Director
Ecole Polytechnique

DAVID JOHNSTON
Principal and Vice Chancellor
McGill University

LEO KRISTJANSON
President
University of Saskatchewan

ARNOLD NAIMARK
President and Vice Chancellor
University of Manitoba

JEAN-GUY PAQUET
Rector
Laval University

WLADIMIR PASKIEVICI
Director of Research
Ecole Polytechnique

GEORGE PEDERSEN
President
University of British Columbia

ROLAND ROUX
Director, Innovation Centre
Ecole Polytechnique

NORMAN WAGNER
President
University of Calgary

UNIVERSITY RESEARCHERS

P.P. BIRINGER
University of Toronto

GREGOR BOCHMAN
University of Montreal

J.K. BRIMACOMBE
University of British Columbia

DON BRODIE
University of Waterloo

DAVID BURNS
University of Waterloo

J.A. CHERRY
University of Waterloo

BETTY CROWN
University of Alberta

IRWIN DIENER
University of Alberta

R.R. HAERING
University of British Columbia

DAVID HOLDEN
University of Waterloo

GEORGE KHACHATOURINAS
University of Saskatchewan

HUGH LAWFORD
University of Toronto

E.S. LEE
University of Toronto

GEORGE LEE
University of Saskatchewan

JASPER MCKEE
University of Manitoba

TONY NOUJIM
University of Alberta

EDO NYLAND
University of Alberta

JACQUELINE SEGALL
University of Toronto

DON SPINK
University of Waterloo

TIM TOPPER
University of Waterloo

MICHELL WINNIK
University of Toronto

MAX WONG
McMaster University

OTHERS

JOHN BRADFIELD
Senior Bursar Trinity College
Cambridge University

RICHARD CUTTING
Managing Director
Sinclair Research
Cambridge, England

RICHARD FOSTER
Director
Management of Technology—
  Practice Leader
McKinsey & Company
New York

ARTHUR H. HEADLAM
Director of Research Services
University of Waterloo

CARLOS E. KRUYTBOSCH
Staff Associate
Office of Planning and Policy Analysis
National Science Foundation
Washington, D.C.

FLOYD L. LANCE
Manager, Business Affairs
Optical Sciences Center
The University of Arizona

FRANK LONGO
Research Associate
Science Council of Canada

KRISTIAN S. PALDA
School of Business
Queen's University

ROSS PERRY
Director of Policy Analysis
IDEA Corporation

CHARLES H. PEYTON
Associate Vice President for Research
The University of Arizona

GRAHAM PLOWS
Chief Executive Officer
Lintech Instruments
Cambridge, England

H.C. ROWLINSON
*Vice President of
  Research and Technology*
C-I-L Inc.

NICK SEGAL
Partner
Segal, Quince and Associates
Cambridge, England

A. STEVEN WALLECK
Director
Manufacturing—Practice Leader
McKinsey & Company
Cleveland, Ohio

APPENDIX B

Members of the Forum 1984-85

EXECUTIVE COMMITTEE

Chairman

LLOYD I. BARBER
President and Vice-Chancellor
University of Regina

Deputy Chairman

ALLAN R. TAYLOR
President & Chief Operating Officer
The Royal Bank of Canada

Co-Founders
& Vice-Chairmen

DAVID E. ALLNUT

GERALD C. GUMMERSELL
Concordia University

Members

GEORGE E. CONNELL
President
University of Toronto

DONALD K. MCIVOR
Chairman & CEO
Imperial Oil Limited

J.V. RAYMOND CYR
Chairman & C.E.O.
Bell Canada

JOHN H. PANABAKER
Chairman
The Mutual Life Assurance
Company of Canada

JAMES DOWNEY
President & Vice-Chancellor
University of New Brunswick

JEAN-GUY PAQUET
Rector
Université Laval

GENERAL MEMBERSHIP

ALLAN K. ADLINGTON,
Acting President,
University of Western Ontario

ROBERT A. BANDEEN,
Chairman & CEO,
Crown Life Insurance Company

LAURENT BEAUDOIN,
Chairman & CEO,
Bombardier Inc.

WILLIAM E. BECKEL,
President & Vice-Chancellor,
Carleton University

JAMES T. BLACK,
Chairman & CEO,
The Molson Companies

GILLES BOULET,
President,
Université du Québec

WILLIAM E. BRADFORD,
Deputy Chairman,
Bank of Montreal

ALTON S. CARTWRIGHT,
Chairman & CEO,
Canadian General Electric Co. Ltd.

ALEX CURRAN,
President,
SED Systems Inc.

C. WILLIAM DANIEL,
President & CEO,
Shell Canada Limited

A. JEAN DE GRANDPRÉ,
Chairman & CEO,
Bell Canada Enterprises Inc.

ANTOINE D'IORIO,
Rector & Vice-Chancellor,
University of Ottawa

ROWLAND C. FRAZEE,
Chairman & CEO,
The Royal Bank of Canada

JEAN-PAUL GOURDEAU,
President & CEO,
The SNC Group

CLAUDE HAMEL,
Rector,
Université de Sherbrooke

LESLIE HARRIS,
President & Vice-Chancellor,
Memorial University

MYER HOROWITZ,
President & Vice-Chancellor,
University of Alberta

RONALD W. IANNI,
President & Vice-Chancellor,
University of Windsor

DAVID L. JOHNSTON,
Principal & Vice-Chancellor,
McGill University

PATRICK J. KENNIFF,
Rector & Vice-Chancellor,
Concordia University

LEO F. KRISTJANSON,
President & Vice-Chancellor,
University of Saskatchewan

PAUL LACOSTE,
Rector,
Université de Montréal

RADCLIFFE R. LATIMER,
President & CEO,
TransCanada PipeLines

JEAN-CLAUDE LEBEL,
Chairman & CEO,
Le Groupe SGF

J. MAURICE LECLAIR,
President & CEO,
Canadian National

ALVIN A. LEE,
President & Vice-Chancellor,
McMaster University

WALTER F. LIGHT,
Chairman,
Northern Telecom Limited

H. IAN MACDONALD,
Chairman,
IDEA Corporation

GORDON F. MACFARLANE,
Chairman & CEO,
British Columbia Telephone Co.

W. ANDREW MACKAY,
President & Vice-Chancellor,
Dalhousie University

BURTON C. MATTHEWS,
President & Vice-Chancellor,
University of Guelph

DAVID MCCAMUS,
President & CEO,
Xerox Canada Inc.

DAVID E. MITCHELL,
President & CEO,
Alberta Energy Company Ltd.

DAVID MORTON,
President & CEO,
Aluminum Company of Canada Ltd.

ARNOLD NAIMARK,
President & Vice-Chancellor,
University of Manitoba

ARNE R. NIELSEN,
Chairman & CEO,
Canadian Superior Oil Limited

K. GEORGE PEDERSEN,
President & Vice-Chancellor,
University of British Columbia

HOWARD E. PETCH,
President,
University of Victoria

PAUL PHOENIX,
President,
Dofasco Inc.

ROBERT P. PURVES,
President,
Inter-Ocean Grain Company Ltd.

JOHN D. REDFERN,
Chairman & CEO,
Canada Cement Lafarge Limited

WILLIAM G. SAYWELL,
President & Vice-Chancellor,
Simon Fraser University

DAVID C. SMITH,
Principal & Vice-Chancellor,
Queen's University

WILLIAM W. STINSON,
President,
Canadian Pacific Limited

WILLIAM I.M. TURNER,
Chairman & CEO,
Consolidated Bathurst Inc.

NORMAN E. WAGNER,
President & Vice-Chancellor,
University of Calgary

DOUGLAS T. WRIGHT,
President & Vice-Chancellor,
University of Waterloo

HONORARY MEMBER

JOHN W. O'BRIEN,
Rector-Emeritus,
Concordia University

COUNSEL

WILLIAM T. MCCONNELL,
Partner,
Peat Marwick & Partners

JAMES A. ROBB, QC,
Senior Partner,
Stikeman, Elliott

STAFF

PATRICIA ROMAN,
Executive Coordinator

MAUREEN DANINO,
Secretary-Receptionist

APPENDIX C

Selected Bibliography

"A Technology Lag that May Stifle Growth," *Business Week*, October 11, 1982.

Anderson, Ronald, "Canada's R&D Incentives Greater than Other Countries," *The Globe and Mail*, April 8, 1983.

"Attracting the Research Dollar," *The New York Times*, March 9, 1985.

Baltare, Carl W. "Framework for Research and Development," *CA Magazine*, March 1981.

Bell, John. "The Back Door to British Research," *New Scientist*, December 20, 1984.

Bhaneja, B., *et al. Technology Transfer by Department of Communications: A Study of Eight Innovations*. Ottawa: Ministry of State for Science and Technology, 1980.

Bird, Richard M. and Meyer W. Bucovetsky. *Private Support for Universities*. Toronto: Commission on the Future Development of the Universities of Ontario, October 1984.

"Bonn's Late Push in the High-Tech Race," *Business Week*, April 9, 1984.

Bourgault, Pierre and Harold Crookell. "Commercial Innovation in Secondary Industry," *Business Quarterly*, Autumn 1979.

"Brief Outlines Problems Facing University R&D," *Canadian Research*, April 1984.

Bueckert, Dennis. "Adapt New Ways to Create Jobs Science Boss Says," *Toronto Star*, November 5, 1984.

Bullock, Matthew. *Academic Enterprise, Industrial Innovation, and the Development of High Technology Financing in the United States.* London: Brand Brothers, 1983.

Burrows, Jean. "New Directions at C-I-L: Research Efforts to Reflect Changing Needs of Markets," *Canadian Research*, February 1985.

Cadbury, Sir Adrian. "Technological Innovation: University Roles." Keynote address to the 13th Commonwealth Universities Congress, August 15, 1983.

"Canada Counts on Other People's Money," *The Economist*, November 3, 1984.

"Canada's R&D Effort," *The Financial Times of Canada*, July 30, 1984.

Canadian Federation of Independent Business. *A Study of Job Creation 1975 to 1982 and Forecasts to 1990*, 1983.

Chakrabarti, Alok K., Stephen Feineman, and William Fuentevilla. "Characteristics of Sources, Channels, and Contents for Scientific and Technical Information Systems in Industrial R&D," *IEEE Transactions on Engineering Management*, May 1983.

Chand, U.K. Ranga. "Innovation and Its Environment," *The Canadian Business Review*, Autumn 1980.

--------- and Susan D. Simeon. *Research and Development in the Canadian Corporate Sector: A Survey of Attitudes and Spending Intentions.* Ottawa: Conference Board of Canada, 1984.

Chevreau, Jonathan. "Omnibus, Waterloo Combine to Develop 3-D Film Software," *The Globe and Mail*, August 31, 1984.

Chisholm, Donald. "Business as the Broker Between Science, Society," *The Financial Post*, May 14, 1984.

Cochrane, W.A. *University/Industry Interface: Overcoming the Barriers*, Speech to the Canadian Council of University Biology Chairman, November 18, 1982.

De Melto, Dennis P., Kathryn E. McMullen, and Russel M. Willis. *Preliminary Report: Innovation and Technological Change in Five Canadian Industries*, Ottawa: Economic Council of Canada, October 1980.

De Young, H. Garrett. "Can Europe Catch Up in the Technology Race?" *High Technology*, October 1984.

Diamond, Edwin and Norman Sandler. "Technology and the Candidates," *High Technology*, October 1984.

Dimancescu, Dan. "High Tech: How Big? What Next?" *High Technology*, October 1984.

Dorfman, Nancy S. "Route 128: The Development of a Regional High Technology Economy," *Research Policy*, 1983.

Ecklund, Christopher S. and Judith H. Dobrzynski. "Merck: Pouring Money into Basic Research to Replace an AGing Product Line," *Business Week*, November 26, 1984.

Economic Council of Canada. *The Bottom Line: Technology, Trade and Income Growth*. Ottawa: Supply and Services Canada, 1983.

----------. "Companies Should Disclose R&D Spending," *Au Courant*, Vol. 4, No. 4, 1984.

European Management Forum. *Report on International Industrial Competitiveness, 1984*. Geneva: Business Press International, 1984.

Fortier, Claude. "Supporting R&D in Isolation is Like Building a One-Legged Stool - A Futile Exercise," *Canadian Business*, March 1981.

----------. "University-Industry Interaction," in *Science Council of Canada Annual Review, 1981*. Ottawa: Supply and Services, 1981.

Geldens, Max. "Towards Fuller Employment: We Have Been Here Before," *The Economist*, July 28, 1984.

Good, Mary Lowe. "Industrial Research is Inefficient and Chaotic, But it Works," *Industrial Research and Development*, November 1982.

Greenspon, Edward. "Saskatchewan Venture-Capital Plan Could By-Pass the Small Investor," *The Financial Post*, July 7, 1984.

Hay, Keith A.J and Robert J. Davies. "Declining Resources, Declining Markets," *International Perspectives*, March/April 1984.

Hicks, Wayland R. "A New Approach to Product Develoment," *High Technology*, October 1984.

"High Technology: The Southeast Reaches Out for Growth Industry," *Economic Review*, September 1983.

Horowitz, Myer. "Look at Mistakes and Learn from Them," *The Financial Post*, May 14, 1984.

"How Business Can Help Universities," *The Financial Post*, October 27, 1984.

Innes, Eva. "Give and Take Needed to Bridge Gap," *The Financial Post*, May 14, 1984.

Irvine, John and Ben R. Martin. *Foresight in Science: Picking the Winners*. London: Frances Pinter, 1984.

"Japan is Buying Its Way into U.S. University Labs," *Business Week*, September 21, 1984.

Joglekar, Prafulla and Morris Hamburg. "An Evaluation of Federal Policies Concerning Joint Ventures for Applied Research and Development," *Management Science*, September 1983.

----------. "An Evaluation of Federal Policy Instruments to Stimulate Basic Research in Industry," *Management Science*, September 1983.

"Joint Venture to Help Students Keep up With New Technology," *The Financial Post*, May 5, 1984.

Keyworth, George A. "Science and Technology Policy: The Next Four Years," *Technology Review*, February/March 1985.

Knight, Michael. "Taxes Hurt Massachusetts Jobs," *The New York Times*, March 26, 1979.

"Leading R&D Spenders in Canada," *The Financial Post*, May 5, 1984.

Light, Walter. "Without R&D Investment, World Competition Impossible," *Computing Canada*, May 26, 1983.

Little, Bruce. "Broader View of R&D Policy Urged," *The Globe and Mail*, August 29, 1984.

Longo, Frank. *Industrial R&D and Productivity in Canada*. Ottawa: Science Council of Canada, May 1984.

Lopata, Roger. "Research Triangle a Far Out Concept that Worked," *Iron Age*, November 23, 1981.

MacAulay, James B. and Paul Dufour. *The Machine in the Garden: The Advent of Industrial Research Infrastructure in the Academic Milieu*. Science Council of Canada, Ottawa, Discussion Paper, March 1984.

Macdonald, H. Ian. "A Five-Point Plan for Commercializing University Research in Ontario." Statement to the Commission on the Future Development of the Universities of Ontario, September 21, 1984.

Macrae, Norman. "Into Intrapreneurial Britain," *The Economist*, February 16, 1985.

Maguire, Carmel and Robin Kench. "Sources of Ideas for Applied University Research, and Their Effect on the Application of Findings in Australian Industry," in *Social Studies of Science*, Vol. 14, London: SAGE, 1984.

Mandel, Ernest. *The Second Slump*. London: Verso, 1980.

Martin, Ben, John Irvine, and Roy Turner. "The Writing on the Wall for British Science," *New Scientist*, November 8, 1984.

Matas, Robert. "Universities Expand Search for Funds Industry's Role in Research Questioned," *The Globe and Mail*, April 16, 1983.

Maxwell, Judith and Stephanie Currie. *Partnership for Growth: Corporate—University Cooperation in Canada*. Montreal: Corporate-Higher Education Forum, 1984.

McPherson, James A. "How Universities Sell Themselves Short." *Canadian Research*, October 1983.

McQuaig, Linda. "Little Scrutiny of Research Plans: Scientists Worried About Tax Break," *The Globe and Mail*, June 11, 1984.

Mensch, Gerhard O. *Stalemate in Technology: Innovations Overcome the Depression*. Cambridge, MA: Ballinger, 1975.

Morantz, Alan. "The Nurturing of R&D: A Good Harvest Takes Management Skill," *Executive*, May 1984.

Moriarity, Andrew. "Wright Report Review: Government Could Improve Technology Development Efforts," *Canadian Research*, February 1985.

National Science Board. *Selected Studies in University Industry Research Relationships*. Washington, D.C., October 1982.

National Science Foundation. *National Patterns of Science and Technology Resources 1984*. Washington, D.C., February 1984.

----------, Office of the General Counsel. "Report on a National Science Foundation Workshop in Intellectual Property Rights in Industry-University Cooperative Research, April 27, 1981", in *University-Industry Research Relationships*, 1982.

----------. *University-Industry Research Relationships ... Myths, Realities and Potentials*, 14th Annual Report of the National Science Board, 1982.

Natural Sciences and Engineering Research Council. *Research Talent in the Natural Sciences and Engineering: Supply and Demand Projections to 1990*. Ottawa, May 1985.

Nelson, Barry. "Bugs for Snow May Aid the Fight Against Frost," *The Globe and Mail*, December 14, 1984.

Norris, William C. "Cooperative R&D: A Regional Strategy," *Issues in Science and Technology*, National Academy of Sciences, Washington, D.C., Winter 1985.

Nowlan, David M. and Richard Bellaire, Eds. *Financing Canadian Universities: For Whom and By Whom?* University of Toronto: Institute for Policy Analysis, 1983.

Office of Research, University of Guelph. *The Industrial Interaction Strategy of the University of Guelph*, March 1982.

Ontario, Ministry of Industry and Trade. *The Technology Challenge: Ontario Faces the Future*, Toronto, June 1984.

Organization for Economic Co-operation and Development. *New Forms of Co-operation and Communication Between Industry and Universities: Analytical Report*. Paris, November 1984.

----------. *Specialisation and Competitiveness in High, Medium, and Low R&D Intensity Manufacturing Industries*. Paris, October 1984.

Palda, Kristian S. "Technological Intensity: Concepts and Measurement," Queen's University Working Paper 84.20. Kingston, October 1984.

---------- and Bohumir Pazderka. *Approaches to an International Comparison of Canada's R&D Expenditures*. Ottawa: Economic Council of Canada, 1982.

"Paying the Piper for U.S. Research,"*Business Week*, October 1, 1984.

"The Pitfalls of Trying to Promote Innovation," *The Economist*, June 26, 1982.

Polanyi, Margaret. "Private Funds No Cure for Universities: Study," *The Globe and Mail*, October 27, 1984.

"Private Sector Awakening to Fact it Must Make More R&D Investment," *The Financial Post*, October 27, 1984.

"Research and Development Outlays Overdone," *The Globe and Mail*, May 11, 1984.

"Research, Development Rank as a Low Priority," *The Wall Street Journal*, February 1, 1984.

"Review: Picking the Winners in the Research Lottery," *New Scientist*, November 22, 1984.

Riche, Richard W., Daniel E. Hecker, and John U. Burgan. "High Technology Today and Tomorrow: A Small Slice of the Employment Pie," *Monthly Labor Review*, November 1983.

Rodger, David. "Haering is the Spark Plug Behind Moli Rechargeable," *Computer Post, The Financial Post Special Report*, Winter 1984.

Rugman, Alan M. and John McIlveen. "The Strategic Management of Canada's Multinationals: Who Needs High Tech?" *Business Quarterly*, Fall 1984.

Schmitt, Roland W. "National R&D Policy: An Industrial Perspective," *Science*, Vol. 224, June 15, 1984.

Science Council of Canada. *Canadian Industrial Development: Some Policy Directions*, Report #37. Ottawa: September 1984.

"Science Parks, Financial Times Survey," *The Financial Times*, October 1, 1984.

Science Policy Research Unit, University of Sussex. *Success and Failure in Industrial Innovation*. Report on Project Sappho. February 1972.

"Silicon Valley Guessing Game," *The Economist*, December 15, 1984.

Skolnik, Michael L and Norman S. Rowen. *"Please, Sir, I Want Some More"—Canadian Universities and Financial Restraint*. Toronto: OISE, 1984.

Smith, Stuart L. "Getting Canada to Jump into the High-Value World," *The Globe and Mail*, December 20, 1984.

Sprung, J.P. "The Business of Software Licensing at the University of Waterloo," *Journal of the Society of Research Administrators*, Vol. XV, No. 2, Fall 1983.

Steklasa, Robert. "High-Technology Know-How Puts Waterloo on R&D Map," *The Financial Post*, December 10, 1983.

----------. "More Firms Marrying Up with Labs in Universities." *The Financial Post*, October 1, 1983.

Strauss, Stephen. "Shortcut Could Lead to Cheaper Antibiotics," *The Globe and Mail*, December 17, 1984.

Supapol, A.B. and D.G. McFetridge. "An Analysis of the Federal Make-or-Buy Policy." Economic Council of Canada, Discussion Paper No. 217, Ottawa, June 1982.

Szuprowicz, Bohdan O. "Battle Lines Being Drawn for Global Technology Markets," *High Technology*, October 1984.

Tamaribuchi, Kay. "Effectively Linking Industry with a University Resource: A Survey of University-Industry Liaison Programs." *Proceedings: Management of Technological Innovation: Facing the Challenge of the 1980's*. Washington, D.C. 1983.

Tanzer, Andrew. "The Silicon Valley Greater Co-prosperity Sphere," *Forbes*, December 17, 1984.

"Technology the French Way," *The Economist*, November 17, 1984.

Tefft, Marianne. "Universities are Caught in Financial Whirlpool," *The Financial Post*, October 20, 1984.

"The Tempest Raging Over Profit-Minded Professors," *Business Week*, November 7, 1983.

Tucker, Jonathan B. "R&D Consortia: Can U.S. Industry Beat the Japanese at Their Own Game?" *High Technology*, October 1984.

"Universities, Industries Look More to Co-op Projects," *The Financial Post*, May 5, 1984.

University of Calgary Technology Transfer Committee. "Expanding Horizons: Strategy for the Transfer of University Research and Innovation," June 1983.

Watson, William G. "Universities Should Keep Their Distance," *The Financial Post*, November 10, 1984.

"What's Ahead in Technology . . . Blind Spot in Strategic Planning," *Management Review*, October 1984.

Wright, Douglas, *et al. Report of the Task Force on Federal Policies and Programs for Technology Development*. Ottawa: Ministry of State for Science and Technology, 1984.

Yulsman, Tom. "The 100: Who They Are and What They Think," *Science Digest*, December 1984.

Zielinski, Andy. "Alberta's $8.6 Million Leduc Research Facility," *Food in Canada*, February 1985.